The University and the City

A Centennial View
of the
University of Chicago

The University of Chicago Library 1992

Front Flyleaf: Boating in Jackson Park, 1905.

Frontispiece: State Street looking north from Randolph, 1911.

Page vi: Frank Lloyd Wright's Robie House at Woodlawn Avenue and 58th Street, undated.

Page viii: Railroad yards south of the Loop, 1912.

Back Flyleaf: Sheep grazing in Washington Park, 1906.

Produced by Kim Coventry
Edited by Daniel Meyer
Designed by Joan Sommers
Centennial series design by William Seabright and Associates
Printed by Dupli-graphic Processors on Vintage Velvet

Text set in Walbaum Roman, Display in Radiant Medium,
and Initial Letters in Radiant Bold Extra Condensed

Cover photograph: Architectural detail, east facade, Swift Hall.
© Copyright Alan Shortall, 1991.

1,000 copies of this catalogue were published in conjunction with the exhibition, *The University and the City: A Centennial View of the University of Chicago,* held in the Department of Special Collections, the University of Chicago Library, March 26 through June 9, 1992.

CHICAGO

Library of Congress Cataloging-in-Publication Data
   The University and the city: a centennial view of
 the University of Chicago: [exhibition].
      p. cm.
  ISBN 0-943056-17-9
   1. University of Chicago — History — Exhibitions.
   2. Chicago (Ill.) — History — Exhibitions
 I. University of Chicago. Library.
 LD928.U55   1992
 378.773′11′074–dc20   92-6296
                                                              CIP

Contents

Preface

"The University and the City" forms the third in a series of four exhibitions and accompanying catalogues offered in conjunction with the Centennial of the University of Chicago. The relationship between the University and the city of Chicago extends far beyond its name and dates to the very founding of the institution. Donations from all sectors combined to match John D. Rockefeller's promised endowment; this broad base of community support has flourished over the past one hundred years.

By choosing to locate the University within the city of Chicago, the founders committed themselves to an institution whose urban identity was at the core of its character. With the World's Columbian Exposition virtually in its backyard, the University and the city entered the twentieth century together. The development of urban sociology, partly a response to growth and change in the new century, is only one example of how the faculty, in studying topics such as race, ethnicity, education, poverty, and politics, derive a research focus from the city and return to it enriched understanding and active participation.

"The University and the City" examines the intersection of the two institutions through the individuals and issues that brought them together. Civic leaders have always played a major role in the University's governance, serving on the Board of Trustees and providing leadership in fundraising campaigns. As readers of this catalogue and viewers of the exhibition will discover, relationships forged between the University and the city in the realms of commerce, science, religion, education, and culture shaped the life of each. Recognizing these contributions constitutes an important part of the University's Centennial.

The Centennial exhibitions in Special Collections received support from the Office of the President. Jean O'Brien participated in the early research stages of the project. Work on this exhibition and catalogue was begun by Maureen Harp and continued by Ted Fishman, who conducted research and wrote early versions of several sections. Richard Popp performed the research and writing of additional sections and assisted in editing the catalogue and developing the exhibition. All of these activities were directed by Daniel Meyer, who also edited the catalogue. His effort and expertise ensured the successful completion of the project, and they are warmly acknowledged. Kim Coventry coordinated the design and production of the exhibition and the publication of the catalogue.

Alice Schreyer
Curator
Department of Special Collections

Introduction

When the University of Chicago opened in 1892, American cities were in the midst of a period of remarkable growth and change. As new industries expanded, trade and services diversified, and the tide of recent immigrants swelled into the millions, cities achieved an unprecedented size and density that shifted the focus of American society from rural farms and towns to the urban street.

William Rainey Harper and other university leaders recognized that the growing force of urbanization had profound implications for the future of American higher education. Speaking at Nicholas Murray Butler's inauguration as president of Columbia University in 1902, Harper saw the potential for nothing less than a complete institutional transformation. "A university which will adapt itself to urban influence," said Harper, "which will undertake to serve as an expression of urban civilization, and which is compelled to meet the demands of an urban environment will in the end become something essentially different from a university located in a village or small city.... It will gradually take on new characteristics both outward and inward, and it will ultimately form a new type of university."

For Harper, the model of the new urban American university was the University of Chicago, the comprehensive research institution he had outlined in his first *Official Bulletin* of 1890 and continued to shape over the next fifteen years as president. In its combination of graduate and undergraduate studies, diversity of curricular offerings and degree programs, and efficient four-quarter academic calendar, the University reflected the enlarged scale and quickened tempo of twentieth-century urban life.

More than this, in Harper's imagination the University was to be the focal point of a network of academies, schools, and colleges, each of them feeding promising students to the University and serving as part of a larger, integrated educational system. In the realm of higher education, the University would thus parallel the role and influence of the city of Chicago, which through its banks, commodities markets, industries, and railroads dominated commerce in the Middle West and claimed a central role in directing the economic growth of the nation. Harper's ambition for the systematic coordination of every form of education and its integration with the life of the city extended to those who were not able to become full-time students on the University campus. An extension division offered academic instruction by mail, and with the needs of those who lived in the city particularly in mind, public lectures were offered in a variety of neighborhood locations along with a full complement of evening and weekend courses for degree credit.

Harper's visionary program found ready acceptance in Chicago, in part because the city was enjoying an era of expansion and welcomed the exhilaration of big ideas. In the decades around the turn of the century, sprawling plants manufacturing McCormick farm machinery, Pullman sleeper cars, and thousands of other products were making Chicago brand names known across the nation. The meat-packing firms of Armour and Swift were building fortunes on the livestock moving through the pens of the Chicago stockyards. The grand State Street department stores of Marshall Field and Carson Pirie Scott and the thriving mail-order enterprises of Sears, Roebuck and Montgomery Ward were setting

new standards for effective and innovative retailing. The imposing terminal stations and switching yards surrounding the Loop testified to the might of Chicago-owned railroads as they extended their tracks south and west across the prairie. Less conspicuously, but just as significantly, the grain traders, bankers, real estate brokers, shippers, lawyers, and agents who channeled and invested the city's wealth were profiting from a commerce that they felt was destined inevitably to grow despite the destruction of urban fires, periodic natural catastrophes, and the persistent cycle of financial boom and panic.

The city of Chicago also welcomed the University because higher education filled an important position in the array of cultural institutions that civic leaders were intent upon building. Older institutions such as the Chicago Historical Society and the Chicago Academy of Sciences were part of this ambitious effort, as was the Art Institute of Chicago. So too were the Chicago Symphony Orchestra, the Chicago Public Library, and the two great privately endowed research collections, the Newberry Library and John Crerar Library. The World's

Columbian Exposition of 1893 was the most spectacular and most ephemeral of these cultural endeavors, its image of classical refinement gone after a single summer. Yet the fair vividly expressed the ideals and expectations of the city's social elite and left its own permanent legacy with the establishment of the Field Columbian Museum, housed in what had been the Fine Arts Building in Jackson Park.

If the city of Chicago was quick to see the benefits a new academic institution would bring, members of the University faculty were equally alert to the advantages of working in a metropolis. Obviously, a large city offered the University a substantial pool of prospective students and the promise of more generous financial support from its patrons. But there were other lures as well. Political economists sought to understand the operation of large industrial concerns. Sociologists were drawn to the problems of immigration, ethnicity, delinquency, and social order. Educators saw an opportunity to test new theories of learning. Social workers wanted to address inequities in employment, child care, and public health. Political scientists were concerned about the corruption of municipal government, the power of party machines, and the future of the democratic system. For scholars in all of these fields and others, the city of Chicago offered an ideal laboratory for investigation, experimentation, and discovery.

In pursuing their urban research, professors from the University soon learned that the city was home to an important array of liberal intellectuals and cultural critics. Rabbi Emil G. Hirsch, an eloquent spokesman for Reform Judaism in Chicago, held a University professorship of rabbinic literature and philosophy. Frank W. Gunsaulus, the pastor of Chicago's popular Central Church and founding president of the Armour Institute of Technology, taught on the Divinity School faculty. Francis W. Parker, the noted educational reformer who headed the Cook County Normal School and the Chicago Institute, joined the University's School of Education in 1901. Many in the University community came to know Chicago settlement leaders such as Jane Addams, Julia Lathrop, Florence Kelley, Mary McDowell, and Graham Taylor and worked with them on research projects and reform campaigns. Writers

from the University shared friendships and journal pages with literary figures from Hamlin Garland and Sherwood Anderson to Carl Sandburg and Harriet Monroe. Faculty associations with Chicago reformers in the arts led to commissioned works from architects such as Tallmadge & Watson, Robert Spencer, Dwight Perkins, the Pond brothers, and Frank Lloyd Wright, who designed a Montana vacation retreat for several University professors.

Important connections were also made with progressive Chicago philanthropists who were prepared to support the research of individual faculty members. Anita McCormick Blaine helped underwrite John Dewey's educational experiments, while Julius Rosenwald encouraged Sophonisba Breckinridge in the creation of the University's school of social work. Helen Culver, who gave Hull House to Jane Addams and whose generosity made possible the Hull Biological Laboratories on the University campus, also funded sociologist W. I. Thomas's pioneering research into the Polish immigrant experience. In these and other ways, the University faculty came to appreciate the level of personal

support that members of the Chicago community were prepared to give.

This pattern of relations was maintained through World War I and the years immediately thereafter, but with the onset of the depression, change began to affect both the city and the University. The south side of the city, where the University was located, felt the cumulative effects of ethnic mobility and shifting patterns of residence. Older buildings in Hyde Park began to show their years, and larger houses and apartments were subdivided for a poorer and less stable residential population.

The academic image of the University as it had been developed within the city was also affected. A new University president, Robert M. Hutchins, became known for his brilliant educational iconoclasm and, especially after the elimination of varsity football on campus, his opposition to traditional American collegiate values. Charles Walgreen, head of a Chicago chain of drug stores, leveled charges that University professors were importing leftist ideologies and imposing them on naive students. The co-founder of the Chicago-based Benton and

Bowles advertising agency, William Benton, was recruited to evaluate the University's public image and recommend effective ways to strengthen and maintain strong relations with the Chicago community. There were conspicuous successes in this effort, particularly with Charles Walgreen, who withdrew his accusations and established a distinguished University lecture series on American institutions and values.

This period of University-city relations culminated with the secret work of the Manhattan Project during World War II. Operating on and near the University campus, scientists created the first controlled, self-sustaining nuclear chain reaction and provided additional research support for the development of the atomic bomb. The close cooperation of the scientific community and the federal government resulted in the postwar creation of the University's Research Institutes. It also led directly to the University's involvement in the development of the Argonne National Laboratory in Du Page County, the beginning of the scientific and technical research and development corridor in the western Chicago suburbs.

In the years after the war, attention shifted to the Hyde Park neighborhood, where city, state, federal, community, and University leaders created one of the nation's earliest comprehensive redevelopment programs. Controversial though it was, urban renewal in Hyde Park successfully determined the character of the community for decades to come and ensured that the University itself would remain a Chicago institution.

Consultation between the University and city officials also encouraged interactions between scholarship and public policy. As technology and social forces transformed the character of the city, the University's scholarship and teaching continued to explore the emerging pattern of the urban community. Faculty members at the University are currently providing expertise on a wide range of local public issues including legal aid, gang violence, aging, poverty, tax policy, job training, housing, demography, education, and medical care.

In exploring the theme of the University and the city, this exhibition can only begin to suggest the variety and strength of the ties that have bound the institution and its urban home. Over the past century, the nature of the relationship has changed as both University and city have developed and matured. In many respects, the city has outgrown its early regional ambitions and assumed an international perspective closer to the academic cosmopolitanism that Harper's University adopted from the beginning. The University's perspective on the city has also changed as scholarly disciplines have shifted and coalesced and sources of financial support have become more diffuse. For both the city and the University, however, the bonds and commitments of the 1890s have proved remarkably resilient. The vision of William R. Harper, Charles L. Hutchinson, Thomas W. Goodspeed, Martin A. Ryerson, and the other Chicago backers of the University was largely realized, even if in ways they could not have anticipated. As the University marks its Centennial, Chicago—the University and the city—can measure the significance of the anniversary on the scale of the founders' achievement.

A City Builds a University

Morgan Hall, Baptist Union Theological Seminary, Morgan Park, Illinois, 1886. Founded by Chicago Baptists in 1865, the Morgan Park seminary became the Divinity School of the new University of Chicago. Photograph by C. D. Mosher.

The Shadow of the Old

The campaign for a new University of Chicago took place under the cloud of failure that had doomed its predecessor. The first University, or the Old University as it was later to be known, was the product of the denominational loyalty and civic pride of Chicago's Baptists, but it could not develop the financial strength to survive the trials of its early years. Chicago Baptists felt the bankruptcy of their university in 1886 as a bitter blow and resolved to rebuild its prospects at the earliest opportunity.

The founding of the Old University had seemed bright with promise. In 1856, Chicago Baptist leaders accepted an offer from Senator Stephen A. Douglas of "a site for a University in the city of Chicago." Douglas was a leading figure in the city and state, general counsel for the Illinois Central Railroad, and two years away from the critical series of debates with his downstate rival Abraham Lincoln. Though not himself a Baptist, Douglas was willing to give land to any group that would found an institution of higher learning and thus promote the continuing commercial and cultural development of the city.

Ten acres for a campus were set aside on the west side of

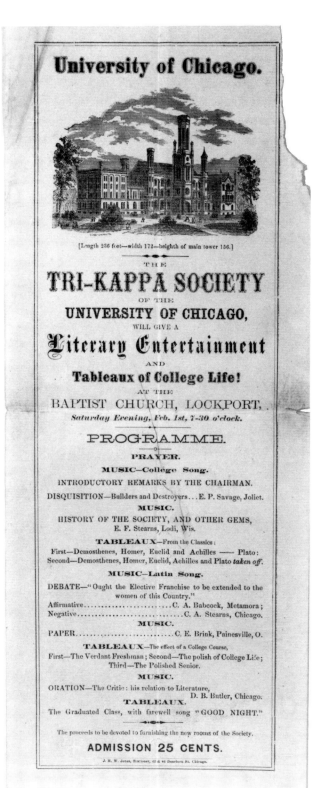

Tri-Kappa Society, Old University of Chicago, handbill, undated. Many students of the Old University were residents of Chicago. After graduation, a large proportion chose to remain in the city, and a few achieved considerable financial success.

Cottage Grove Avenue just north of 35th Street, directly across the road from "Oakenwald," Douglas's expansive lakeshore estate. University leaders confidently anticipated financial support from Douglas and his wealthy friends and hoped that he would deed them the remainder of his land as the institution grew.

The south wing of the Old University's main building was completed in time for the beginning of classes in 1859. Construction was then begun on the main part of the building, Douglas Hall, and on the Dearborn Observatory constructed on its west side, all of which was completed by 1864. In addition to college courses, a preparatory school was established along with medical and law departments. The newly organized Baptist Union Theological Seminary (BUTS) offered its first classes in Douglas Hall in 1867, and the next year it erected its own building adjacent to the campus. For any outside observer, the two institutions seemed ideally situated to reap the benefits of the increasing prosperity of the Baptist community and the steady southward growth of the city of Chicago.

Those inside knew better. Senator Douglas, who was named the first president of the Old University's board of trustees, died in 1861 without providing the institution a bequest. The financial panics of 1857 and 1873 eroded the prosperity of wealthy supporters, both Baptist and non-Baptist, and the great fire of 1871, while leaving the south side of Chicago unscarred, destroyed the commercial heart of the city. The Civil War also disrupted the lives and fortunes of potential donors, and its impact was felt directly when Camp Douglas, one of the Union's largest prisons for captured Confederates, was located just to the north of the Old University grounds.

Faced with growing debt, the BUTS accepted an offer of land from trustee George C. Walker and moved its faculty, students, and library ten miles south to suburban Morgan Park in 1877. The Old University was not so fortunate. Unable to meet its obligations, primarily the debt incurred in erecting Douglas Hall, the institution lost its mortgage to its principal creditor and was forced to close in the spring of 1886.

Baptist leaders in Chicago and throughout the Middle West were humiliated by the extent of the catastrophe. While the BUTS survived in its suburban refuge, the failure of the Old University left the denomination without an academic base to rival the nearby institutional successes of the Presbyterians at Lake Forest College or the Methodists at Northwestern University in Evanston. Resolving to reestablish a Baptist academic presence in Chicago was a group of determined ministers and laymen including George C. Walker, Henry A. Rust, Frederick A. Smith, the Rev. George W. Northrup, president of the BUTS; E. Nelson Blake, president of the Baptist Theological Union; and the Rev. Thomas W. Goodspeed, financial and recording secretary of the board of the BUTS. They shared, Goodspeed wrote later, an "inextinguishable desire and unalterable purpose" that a new institution should emerge from the old. Goodspeed pressed their case with particular urgency on two laymen with close ties to the situation in Chicago: William Rainey Harper, a professor of Semitic languages at Yale who had just left the faculty of the BUTS, and John D. Rockefeller, the Baptist oil magnate who was serving as vice-president of the BUTS board.

The Promise of the New

Within two years of the collapse of the Old University, Chicago Baptists had secured critical denominational support for the creation of a new institution of higher learning in the city. In May 1888, the American Baptist Education Society was formed in Washington, D.C., and Frederick T. Gates, minister of the Central Baptist Church of Minneapolis, was named its corresponding secretary. After surveying the state of Baptist education, Gates quickly became convinced that a new university was needed "in the city of Chicago, and not in a suburb outside the city, but within the city itself and as near its center as conveniently possible."

In May 1889, the Education Society endorsed the Chicago plan and Gates was able to announce momentous news: John D. Rockefeller would give $600,000 toward the endowment of an institution in Chicago if additional pledges of $400,000 could be obtained from other donors before June 1, 1890. The Education Society was swept with enthusiasm, and Gates returned to Chicago with Goodspeed to begin the crucial one-year fundraising campaign.

Gates and Goodspeed recognized that the initial appeal had to be made to Baptists in Chicago and the Middle West. Within sixty days, $200,000 had been raised from within the city, and after nine months of persistent solicitations another $100,000 in pledges had come in from Baptist churches in the region. The remaining $100,000, however, was secured from the non-Baptist business leaders of Chicago whose wealth represented the commercial strength of the city: grain trading, meat packing, dry goods, hardware, shipping, railroads, streetcars, real estate, publishing, and banking. A fourth of the non-Baptist total came from alumni of the Old University, and another fourth from the members of the city's premier Jewish social organization, the Standard Club.

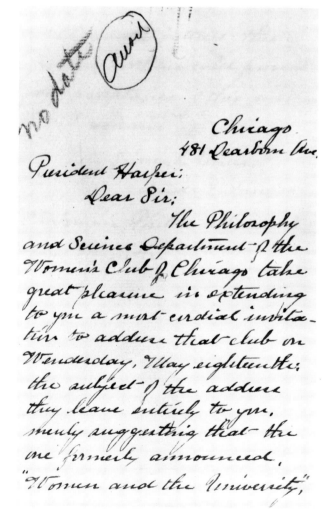

Gertrude P. Dingee to William R. Harper, April 11, 1892. President Harper's persuasive address to Chicago clubwomen created a significant new group of University donors.

Chicago, May 26th '90 188__

F. T. Gates, Cor. Sec.

Dear Sir:--

Satisfied that the con-
ditions attached to the noble pledge of Mr. John
D. Rockefeller to give $600,000 as endowment
for a new institution of learning to be located
in this city have been fulfilled, I take great
pleasure in notifying you that I am prepared
to carry out my covenant of January 22nd, 1890,
to give a site for the new institution and to
furnish further land on the terms suggested.
In common with all citizens of this city, I appreciate the splendid benefaction of Mr. Rockefeller to Chicago. I congratulate the people
of this city and the entire West on the success
achieved, and with all friends of ~~higher~~

culture I rejoice that another noble institution of higher learning is to be founded, and
founded in the heart of the Continent.

Yours very truly,

Marshall Field

Marshall Field to Frederick T. Gates, May 26, 1890. The urban character of the University was confirmed by its site, which lay on the Midway Plaisance only six miles from the center of Chicago and within easy reach of streetcar and railroad lines.

In satisfying the terms of Rockefeller's matching gift within the one-year deadline, the leaders of the new University of Chicago had uncovered a remarkable level of civic support outside denominational bounds. The essential role of the non-Baptist Chicago business community was demonstrated in September 1890, when department store owner Marshall Field, who had given and sold parcels of land on which the University would stand, subscribed his name as one of the institution's six incorporators. The first University Board of Trustees included both Baptists and non-Baptists, among them Charles L. Hutchinson, Martin A. Ryerson, E. Nelson Blake, Ferdinand W. Peck, H. H. Kohlsaat, George C. Walker, Henry A. Rust, Andrew MacLeish, and Eli B. Felsenthal. The nondenominational charac-ter of the University received additional emphasis in 1890-91 when newly elected president William R. Harper began recruit-ing an internationally trained and largely non-Baptist faculty selected on the basis of scholarly distinction.

A trip by Harper to Europe in the summer of 1891 produced another opportunity for Chicago donors to show their generosity. Learning that the entire stock of a long-established Berlin book dealer was available for sale, Harper submitted a purchase offer of $45,000 and returned to Chicago hoping that donors could be found to underwrite the cost. He was not disappointed. Nine Chicago businessmen, including Hutchinson, Ryerson, Kohlsaat, Charles H. McCormick, and Charles R. Crane, pledged the necessary amount, and the University immediately acquired one of the largest academic research collections in the country.

Encouraged by Harper's successes, John D. Rockefeller made a million-dollar gift to the University in late 1890. The next major gift came from Chicago in January 1891, an endowment from the estate of William B. Ogden for a graduate school of scientific research; Ogden had been the mayor of Chicago and for many years the chairman of the Old University's board of trustees. Rockefeller provided an additional million dollars for University operations in February 1892, and his generosity prompted Marshall Field to say, "Now Chicago must put a million dollars into the buildings of the University."

Spurred by a $100,000 challenge gift from Field, a frenetic ninety-day campaign was launched. Money for critically needed University buildings was given by Martin A. Ryerson, George C. Walker, Silas Cobb, and Sidney Kent, and by a new pool of donors representing the women of Chicago: Mrs. Elizabeth Kelly, Mrs. Nancy A. Foster, Mrs. Mary Beecher, Mrs. Henrietta Snell, and members of the Chicago Woman's Club and Fortnightly Club. The campaign was a resounding success, and the University opened in October 1892 with the assurance that through the generosity of Chicago citizens, funds for the classrooms, residence halls, and laboratories essential to its academic work had been secured.

H. N. Higinbotham et al., subscription pledge, June 30, 1892. Marshall Field's initiation of a $1,000,000 challenge campaign for the erection of University buildings prompted ready support from key Chicago businessmen.

The University Neighborhood

Jackson Park promenade, 1903. At the turn of the century, Sunday strollers in Hyde Park could enjoy the pleasures of the Lake Michigan beach and a vista dominated by the tower of the German Pavilion, a relic of the Columbian Exposition.

Hyde Park-Kenwood

Chicago, like other large American cities, expanded rapidly in population in the late nineteenth century. Not all of the growth was confined within municipal boundaries. Taking advantage of swift streetcar and railroad transportation, the middle and upper classes in increasing numbers abandoned urban neighborhoods for the comforts of suburban communities established five or ten miles away from the city's center.

Real estate developer Paul Cornell sensed the importance of this trend and was one of the first in Chicago to promote the lure of suburban life. Planning an ideal commuter village, Cornell bought 300 acres of vacant lakefront land south of Chicago in 1853. Sixty acres were given to the Illinois Central Railroad on the condition that it extend its lines to the new community and build a station at what was to be called Hyde Park. Cornell provided his embryonic village with a church and public parkland. He also built a resort hotel on Lake Michigan at 53rd Street, where vacationing Chicagoans could take in the fresh air and scenery and learn the advantages of purchasing a lot in one of Cornell's nearby subdivisions.

Early residents of Hyde Park and its sister suburb to the north, Kenwood, were quick to provide their communities with the embellishments of a cultivated life. The Hyde Park Literary Society was formed along with the Kenwood Social Club, the Kenwood Tennis Club, the Lyceum, and the Philosophical Society. The Rosalie Music Hall on 57th Street offered a venue for various public meetings, lectures, concerts, and plays.

Within a few years, Chicago had grown large enough to absorb many surrounding sub-urbs, and Hyde Park itself was incorporated within the city in 1889. Now more an urban neighborhood than a suburban village, Hyde Park nonetheless maintained many of its distinctive characteristics. The great South Park system, designed in its original form by Frederick Law Olmsted, gave Hyde Park a magnificent green belt stretching along its southern periphery from Washington Park through the Midway Plaisance to Jackson Park on the lake. The World's Columbian Exposition in Jackson Park and along the Midway in

Kimbark Avenue south from 47th Street, from *Picturesque Kenwood, Hyde Park, Illinois: Its Artistic Homes, Boulevards, Drives, Scenery, and Surroundings* (Chicago: Craig & Messervey, n.d.). Commodious houses and newly planted shade trees epitomized the residential ideal of early Hyde Park and Kenwood.

1893 brought hundreds of thousands of visitors to the south lakeshore, and with them came a real estate boom and substantial residential and retail growth.

The opening of the new University of Chicago in 1892 on the southern edge of Hyde Park assured the community of an additional promotional advantage. Like Lake Forest, Evanston, and other Chicago suburbs, Hyde Park could now benefit from the prestige of an institution of higher education.

The increasing attractiveness of Hyde Park-Kenwood led many of Chicago's wealthiest businessmen, including University trustees Martin A. Ryerson, Harold Swift, and Julius Rosenwald, to build impressive homes in the area. They were joined by prosperous middle-class families and by the great majority of University faculty, who were attracted by comfortable homes in an appealing neighborhood within walking distance of the campus. Their houses were frequently designed by firms with distinguished national and regional reputations: Frank Lloyd Wright, George W. Maher, Holabird & Roche, Wilson & Fox, Marshall & Fox, Alfred Alschuler, and Solon Beman among them.

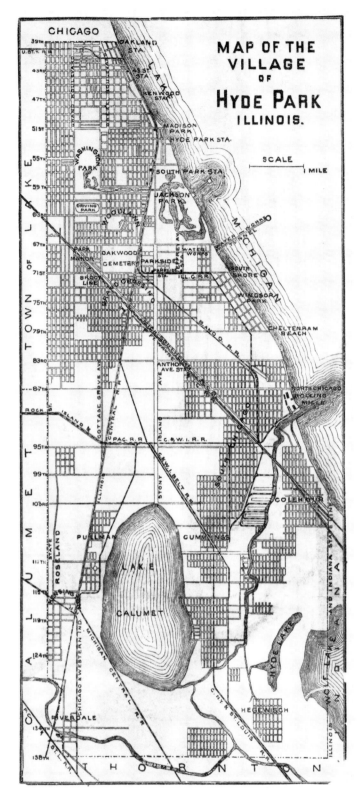

"Map of the Village of Hyde Park, Illinois," 1888. Stephen A. Douglas advised Hyde Park's founder, Paul Cornell, "Whenever you have a spare dollar, plant it between [Chicago] and the Calumet. There the future city will lie." At its greatest extent, the municipality of Hyde Park stretched from State Street to Lake Michigan and from 39th Street to the Indiana border.

A Creative Center

Some of the architects who designed the University's Gothic buildings secured commissions for other work in Hyde Park. Henry Ives Cobb, the University's first architect and the creator of its campus plan, built three houses in Hyde Park in the 1890s, one for President William Rainey Harper. Dwight H. Perkins, whose "Prairie Gothic" design for Hitchcock Hall incorporated ornamentation based on Mid-western fauna, produced three Hyde Park residences. Howard Van Doren Shaw, the fashionable architect of many North Shore estates and the University's Quadrangle Club, executed more than fifteen commissions in the neighborhood, many of them sophisticated adaptations of tra-ditional English manor houses.

Horace B. Mann, one of the principals of Mann, MacNeille & Lindberg and a brother of a University physics professor, led his firm to design four separate complexes of linked rowhouses that came to be called "profes-sors' houses." Bordering shady Hyde Park streets and incorporat-ing all the amenities of comfort-able upper-middle-class life, these rowhouses epitomized the successful integration of a large university into a prosperous residential neighborhood.

Improvements in streetcar lines and more frequent rail service assured Hyde Park's connections with downtown Chicago. By the mid-1920s, the Illinois Central Railroad was running 165 trains daily to and from the neighbor-hood. Except for the area imme-diately around the University campus, Hyde Park's population was increasingly diversified.

First- and second-generation German, Irish, Czech, Italian, and Polish immigrant families moved into the small workers' cottages vacated after the Colum-bian Exposition, while African-Americans found housing in restricted areas near the Illinois Central tracks and along alley-ways. German and Russian Jews, who had migrated south

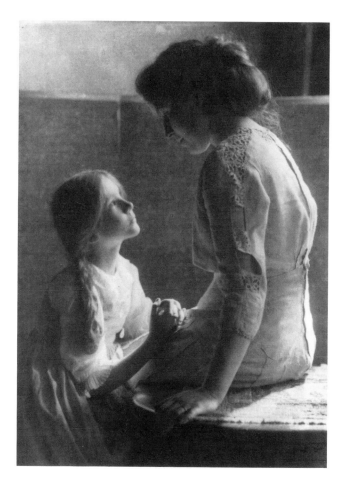

Hanni Steckner Yahrmarkt and her daughter Helga, ca. 1909. A member of the American Photo-Secession movement and the wife of a University professor of German literature, Eva Watson Schütze maintained an active photographic practice in Hyde Park. Photo-graph by Eva Watson Schütze.

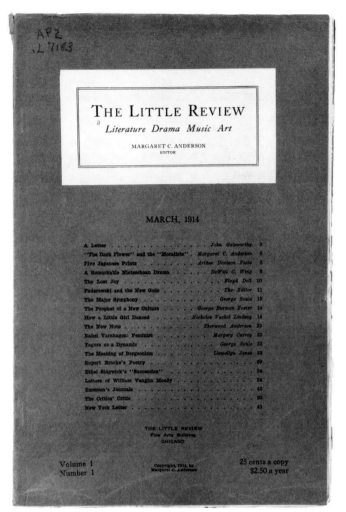

The Little Review, vol. 1, no. 1 (March 1914). One of the most noted of all literary magazines, *The Little Review* was the creation of Margaret Anderson. After announcing its publication at a party given by Floyd Dell, she solicited articles for the first issues from her friends at the 57th Street artists' colony.

from the Loop through a succession of neighborhoods, settled in Hyde Park-Kenwood in large numbers and by the end of the 1930s made up forty percent of the neighborhood's population.

In the early decades of the century, Hyde Park also became a magnet for writers and artists, many of them representing Chicago's cultural avant-garde. In a cluster of wooden buildings along 57th Street and Stony Island Avenue formerly used as souvenir stands during the world's fair, a group of young bohemians congregated around the makeshift residence of writer and artist Floyd Dell. Among the others who became fixtures of this lively artists' colony were Margaret Anderson, founder of the influential *Little Review*; Harriet Monroe, editor of *Poetry* magazine, an assertive voice for modern expression; sometimes controversial realist writers and poets such as Theodore Dreiser, Sherwood Anderson, Edgar Lee Masters, Vachel Lindsay, and Carl Sandburg; and journalists like Ben Hecht who were both participants in and publicists for the new movements in the arts.

Members of the University were among those who frequented the 57th Street colony and attended its readings and informal discussions. Writers Robert Herrick, William Vaughn Moody, and Robert Morss Lovett, all members of the faculty, found common ground with the social, intellectual, and literary concerns of the Chicago bohemians. Divinity School professor George Burman Foster was often seen in the 57th Street shopfronts, where he acquired a nonacademic following as a champion of the philosophy of Nietzsche.

The University, for its part, offered frequent public lectures, concerts, and educational programs and made Hyde Park-Kenwood an attractive neighborhood for professionals with intellectual and cultural interests. Theodore Thomas and Frederick Stock, the first two conductors of the Chicago Symphony Orchestra, were among them. Many of these commuting professionals made their homes in high-rise luxury apartment buildings and residential hotels constructed

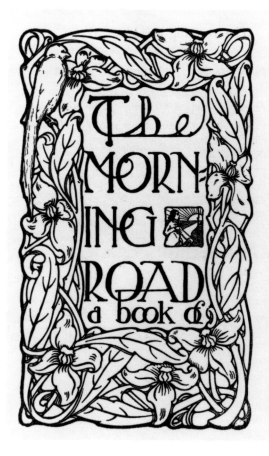

Thomas Wood Stevens and Alden Charles Noble, *The Morning Road: A Book of Verses* (Chicago: Blue Sky Press, 1902), title page. Produced in Kenwood and Hyde Park from 1899 to 1907, the beautifully designed books of the Blue Sky Press were a faithful expression of Arts and Crafts ideals.

between the Illinois Central tracks and the lakeshore or in substantial houses on side streets near the University campus.

Clarence Darrow, America's most celebrated defense attorney, lived in the Midway Apartment Hotel on 60th Street near Stony Island Avenue from his early days of practice as a corporate lawyer until his death in 1938. Among his notable cases was the 1924 defense of Nathan Leopold and Richard Loeb, two Kenwood youths who were convicted of the premeditated murder of Bobby Franks, a neighborhood schoolboy. For Darrow, the University and the Hyde Park community provided an ideal intellectual environment in which to learn and test unconventional ideas. His home was a gathering place for University scholars and others who constituted an informal "biology club" that met to discuss current developments in biology, psychology, anthropology, geology, astronomy, and biblical interpretation.

Based perhaps on their spirited encounters in the biology club, Darrow and George Burman Foster met in 1919 for a series of public debates on religion at the Garrick Theater in Chicago's Loop. Later, in the 1930s, Darrow debated one of the University's most popular

Hyde Park Remembered

lecturers, his long-time friend, anthropologist Frederick Starr, on the topic, "Has the Human Race Justified Its Existence?" The biology club also served as a source of support for Darrow in 1925 during the famous "Monkey Trial" in Dayton, Tennessee. Backing Darrow's successful defense of John Scopes and evolutionary theory were expert witness statements prepared by three friends on the University faculty: zoologist Horatio H. Newman, educator Charles H. Judd, and anthropologist Fay-Cooper Cole.

A SELECTION OF WORKS BY TWENTIETH CENTURY ARTISTS

THE RENAISSANCE SOCIETY
OF
THE UNIVERSITY OF CHICAGO
JUNE 20 TO AUGUST 20, 1934

"A Selection of Works by Twentieth Century Artists," Renaissance Society, exhibition catalogue, 1934. Founded in 1915 by members of the University of Chicago faculty, the Renaissance Society in its early decades became the principal venue for the introduction of twentieth-century art to Chicago.

From 1920 through the era of urban renewal in the 1950s, Hyde Park began to experience the changes that were affecting all large cities in the Northeast and Midwest. Shifting patterns of economic growth, the burgeoning of far-distant suburbs, the great migration of African-Americans from the rural South, and the incipient flight of middle- and upper-class whites from the city all started to have their cumulative effect. Throughout these decades, Hyde Park maintained its reputation as a lively neighborhood that offered gracious living, a diversity of services, and the opportunity for spirited encounters with the latest in the arts and entertainment.

In 1986, Thomas Park, Professor Emeritus of Biology at the University, offered his reminiscences of the neighborhood where he had lived since 1920:

I have a recollection of Hyde Park as a place that's been very green ... From the beautiful array of elm trees on the Midway throughout the whole of Hyde Park ... and Kenwood and all of Jackson Park, there's

a very strong recollection in my mind of wonderful leafing and flowering.

Another impression I had of Hyde Park was its tidy quality ... there was very little litter.

Sunday Matinee Dance ticket, Midway Gardens, 1927. One of Frank Lloyd Wright's most inventive designs, Midway Gardens combined striking modern architecture with the relaxed ambience of a traditional German beer garden. While Prohibition brought an end to public drinking, Midway Gardens continued to offer ballroom dancing into the late 1920s.

Graffiti was an unknown event. We did have one source of filth ... coal dust, because most of Hyde Park was fired for many years with coal furnaces ... you could feel the coal dust everywhere, on your face and on your person and in your books and in your possessions. It was a great blessing when Hyde Park converted from coal to oil. I think the thing I remember most pleasantly about Hyde Park both as a boy and as a young man and as an older man was the quality and diversity of the shops. In [the 1930s and 1940s] one could start at the corner of Lake Park Avenue and 55th Street and walk to Cottage Grove ... and one could find two movie houses, the Jefferson and the Frolic. In somewhat later years, a marvelous pub and jazz emporium called the Beehive, where Miff Mole played. A saloon on the corner known as The Wharf had a very questionable reputation because it was inhabited by many women who blonded their hair ... A few doors down was a very famous old Hyde Park saloon known as Hanley's ... which remained open during Prohibition ... [It] was particularly popular with streetcar motormen and conductors, with truck drivers, and with University professors. It was just filled with University professors during Prohibition.

Shops and restaurants lined 55th Street, including bakeries, a fancy-foods grocery, a butcher, toy shop, several restaurants, the Woodlawn Tap, and the University State Bank. Nightclubs and ballrooms clustered at 63rd Street south of the Midway:

> *At Cottage Grove [and] 63rd Street ... one would find ... the*

Hyde Park residential hotels, from *Hyde Park Then and Now* (Chicago: Hyde Park-Kenwood National Bank, 1929). By the 1920s, the ideal of the single-family suburban villa had given way to the convenience and prestige of the apartment tower.

1. *Jackson Towers.* 2. *"5000 East End."* 3. *Narragansett.* 4. *Cambridge Club.* 5. *Broadview.* 6. *Chicago Beach.* 7. *Shoreland.* These are some of Hyde Park's beautiful hotels. The other page shows seven more.

55th Street west from Lake Park Avenue, ca. 1950. In the years before urban renewal, 55th Street was one of the principal shopping and entertainment districts of Hyde Park.

Tivoli Theater, which was a large luxury theater, much like the Chicago Theater. [There was also] the Trianon Ballroom, which was a place where one would go to dance and pick up dates … the Midway Gardens [at 60th and Cottage Grove] was also a dance hall, but of lower repute, which had the great distinction

of bringing [up] a man from New Orleans named King Oliver who brought with him a young trumpet player … named Louis Armstrong. Louis Armstrong used to play there, and some of us would go hear him play. He was superb.

Renewal and Revival

Muriel Beadle, in her memoir, *The Hyde Park-Kenwood Urban Renewal Years* (1964), described the University's neighborhood as having "a kind of mystique that has long affected ... residents, a certainty that its atmosphere is unique, that life is better and more stimulating than anywhere else." A leader in urban development in Hyde Park, she recounts how this feeling of distinction contributed to neighborhood renewal efforts. "It was the preservation of this 'other world' that engaged the emotions and the energies of residents of Hyde Park-Kenwood and gave them the will to do what they have done."

Before 1950, ninety percent of the University's faculty lived within walking distance of campus, but after that point a steady decline set in that lowered the number to seventy percent by 1964. For members of the University community who were committed to remaining residents of Hyde Park-Kenwood, renewal offered the prospect of stabilizing an unpredictable pattern of mobility that threatened the character of the community.

By the late 1940s, economic and demographic changes had worn the social fabric of Hyde

Citizens' Mass Meeting, Hyde Park Community Council, handbill, March 27, 1952. Called to address the issue of increasing neighborhood crime, a meeting of 2,000 Hyde Park residents at Mandel Hall led to the formation of the South East Chicago Commission.

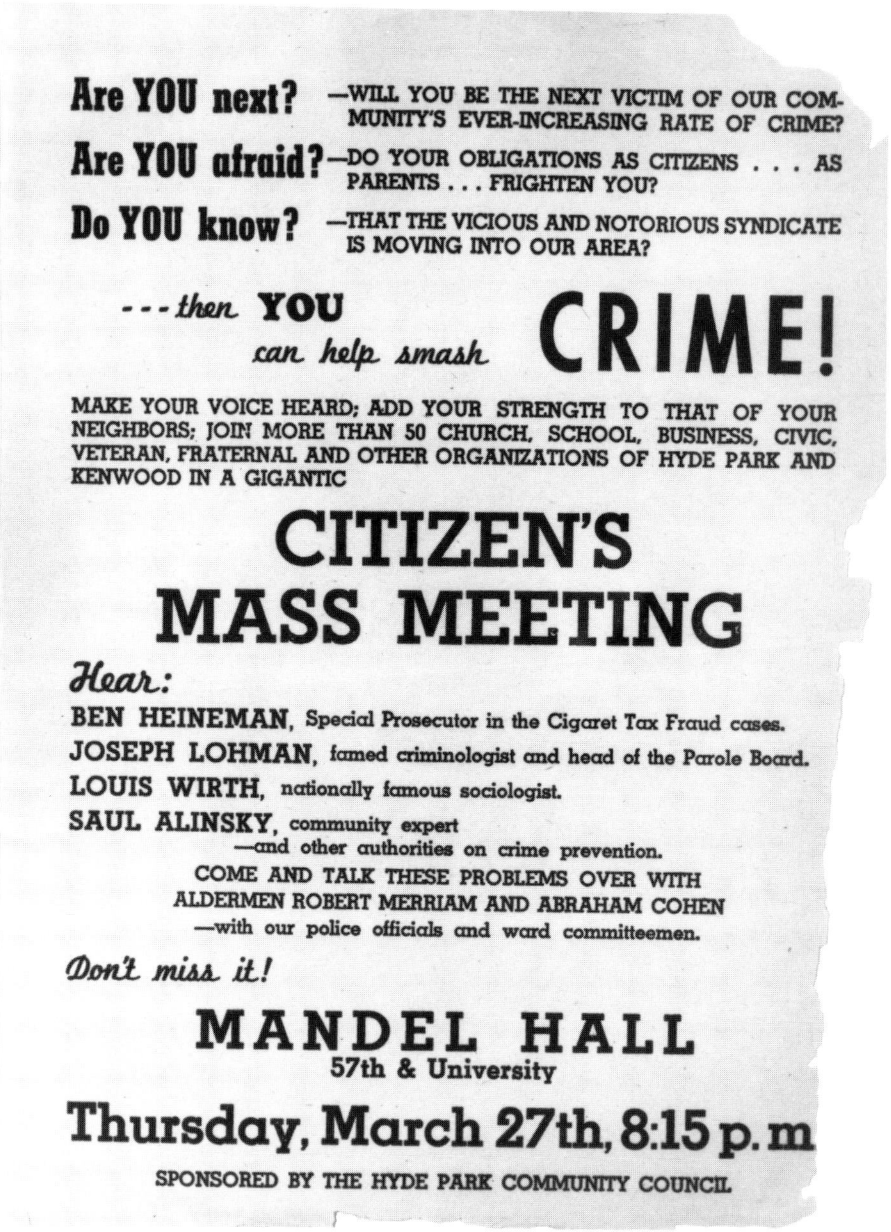

Are YOU next? —WILL YOU BE THE NEXT VICTIM OF OUR COMMUNITY'S EVER-INCREASING RATE OF CRIME?

Are YOU afraid? —DO YOUR OBLIGATIONS AS CITIZENS . . . AS PARENTS . . . FRIGHTEN YOU?

Do YOU know? —THAT THE VICIOUS AND NOTORIOUS SYNDICATE IS MOVING INTO OUR AREA?

--- *then* **YOU** *can help smash* **CRIME!**

MAKE YOUR VOICE HEARD; ADD YOUR STRENGTH TO THAT OF YOUR NEIGHBORS; JOIN MORE THAN 50 CHURCH, SCHOOL, BUSINESS, CIVIC, VETERAN, FRATERNAL AND OTHER ORGANIZATIONS OF HYDE PARK AND KENWOOD IN A GIGANTIC

CITIZEN'S MASS MEETING

Hear:

BEN HEINEMAN, Special Prosecutor in the Cigaret Tax Fraud cases.
JOSEPH LOHMAN, famed criminologist and head of the Parole Board.
LOUIS WIRTH, nationally famous sociologist.
SAUL ALINSKY, community expert
—and other authorities on crime prevention.
COME AND TALK THESE PROBLEMS OVER WITH
ALDERMEN ROBERT MERRIAM AND ABRAHAM COHEN
—with our police officials and ward committeemen.

Don't miss it!

MANDEL HALL
57th & University

Thursday, March 27th, 8:15 p.m

SPONSORED BY THE HYDE PARK COMMUNITY COUNCIL

Park-Kenwood, raising fears that the neighborhood would be undermined by the deteriorating property and flight of residents that were already widespread in the surrounding areas. Maintenance of commercial and residential buildings had been postponed during the decade of the depression and the years of World War II. Buildings formerly occupied by middle- and upper-class families had been subdivided into small one- and two-room apartments and allowed to decline. As the density of poor residents rose, so did the problems of poverty and crime.

At the University, administrators faced a sixty percent drop in student applications in the early 1950s and increasing difficulties in recruiting faculty. Rumors spread that the University was considering moving its campus out of Hyde Park. The Board of Trustees and administrators decided to intervene aggressively in the neighborhood before, as President George W. Beadle was to put it, "they ... ended up with a $200 million investment in a slum, without anybody to do research or any students to educate."

Organized action to improve the neighborhood was launched in 1949 with the formation of the

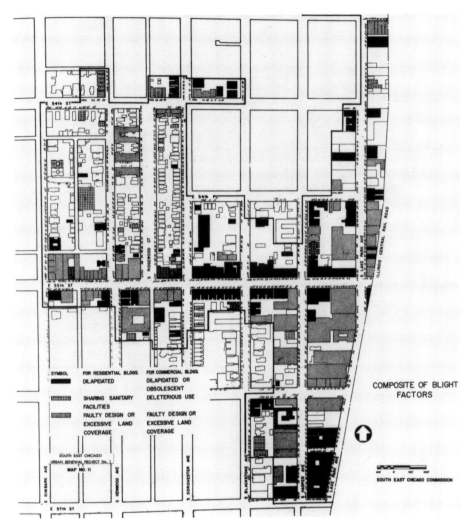

"Composite of Blight Factors," Map no. 11, from *South East Chicago Renewal Project No. 1* (Chicago: South East Chicago Commission, 1954). The urban renewal effort in Hyde Park focused on deteriorated properties bordering 55th Street and Lake Park Avenue.

Hyde Park-Kenwood Community Conference (HPKCC). Drawing heavily for support on local churches and synagogues, the Conference chose a Unitarian minister as its first chairman. From the start, the Conference also maintained an interracial membership and addressed the tensions of race relations along with the problems of housing and crime. The emphasis of its programs was on assuring the neighborhood's future as a stable, prosperous, and integrated community.

17

In 1952, the University made its principal commitment to neighborhood renewal. A mass meeting called to discuss crime resulted in the appointment of a Committee of Five headed by University Chancellor Lawrence A. Kimpton and including community leaders such as Rabbi Louis L. Mann of Sinai Temple. The Committee in turn proposed the creation of a new coordinating organization to deal with the problems of Hyde Park and Kenwood as well as Oakland to the north and Woodlawn to the south. Accordingly, the South East Chicago Commission (SECC) was formed with Chancellor Kimpton as its chairman and Julian H. Levi, a corporate attorney and brother of Law School dean Edward H. Levi, as its executive director. The goals of the SECC were to increase police protection, enforce building codes, promote residential stability, and draw up a plan for the redevelopment of Hyde Park's most seriously deteriorated areas. Although the HPKCC and the SECC were often at odds over matters of policy, they shared a common interest in confronting controversial issues such as poverty, crime, residential displacement, urban planning, and racial integration, which few other urban communities in the early 1950s had addressed.

With a grant from the Field Foundation, the University and SECC created a plan for redevelopment of an extensive area of Hyde Park centered on 55th Street and Lake Park Avenue. This plan was approved by federal, state, and city

Newly constructed townhouses on 56th Street, 1961. In the background, the dual towers of the University Apartments on 55th Street are nearing completion. Photograph by Al Henderson.

Harper Court, John T. Black, architect, perspective drawing, from *Harper Court: A New Center for the Useful Arts ... in the Tradition of Hyde Park* (Chicago: Harper Court Foundation, 1963). Funded with bonds sold to the community, Harper Court was intended to replace artists' quarters lost to urban renewal and provide space for new galleries and "creative enterprises." Muriel Beadle, wife of President George W. Beadle, led the development campaign. Drawing by Human Tan.

governments and received the strong support of Mayor Richard J. Daley. The initial stage of work, demolition of older substandard buildings, began in May 1955. By the summer of 1958, large tracts of land had been cleared, and construction got underway on new apartments, townhouses, and a shopping center.

The Hyde Park neighborhood redevelopment project was expensive and inevitably imperfect. Over 15,000 neighborhood residents were displaced as buildings considered substandard were torn down. Some of Hyde Park's historic nineteenth-century housing stock was lost, and the character of entire blocks and streets in the heart of the neighborhood was completely altered. The cost of the entire redevelopment effort in the area surrounding the University campus exceeded $300 million. The federal government, which regarded Hyde Park as an important testing ground for emerging urgan renewal strategies, provided $46 million for development projects. The University invested $29 million, and an additional $250 million was secured from private investors.

As one of the earliest massive efforts to reshape an American urban neighborhood, the Hyde Park-Kenwood renewal program received its full share of social, political, and architectural criticism. Some of the area's old, familiar graciousness and raucousness would have disappeared over time and could not have been preserved in Hyde Park any more than in any other vigorous city neighborhood. Yet, working in concert, Hyde Park residents and the University were singularly successful in constructing a formula for an economically stable and racially integrated community and in confirming the University's commitment to remain an urban institution.

The Urban Laboratory

Ernest W. Burgess, undated. With Robert Park, Burgess played a central role in defining the urban research program of the "Chicago school" of sociology. Photograph by Paul A. Wagner.

Social Science Research

At the outset, William R. Harper defined the University of Chicago as an institution committed to rigorous standards of research, yet open to the broadest engagement with American society. "Democracy," he wrote, "has scarcely begun to understand itself. It is in the university that the best opportunity is afforded to investigate the movements of the past and to present the facts and principles involved before the public. It is the university that, as the center of thought, is to maintain for democracy the unity so essential for its success."

The important position of the social sciences in this program emerged early in Harper's recruitment of faculty. Albion Small, the president of Colby College, was persuaded to come to Chicago and head an academic department of sociology. Like others Harper recruited, Small seized the opportunity to devote himself to research in his chosen field. "I must put the bulk of my time in on my special work, and in the supervision of courses in . . . Sociology," he wrote. "Our Chicago scheme is the first on this continent to provide for Social Science a chance to be fundamental and comprehensive."

As epitomized by Small, the first generation of social scientists at Chicago saw research as a tool for the promotion of reform. An ordained Baptist minister, Small favored secular scholarship over the pulpit. Nonetheless, like Biblical scholar Harper, he shared liberal Protestant expectations that scientific research into the problems of society would lay the path to a more equitable American democracy. In the first issue of the *American Journal of Sociology*, which he founded, Small wrote, "I would have American scholars, especially in the social sciences, declare their independence of do-nothing traditions. I would have them repeal the law of custom which bars marriage of thought with action." Sharing the pages of the *Journal* in the early years were other reformers with strong religious backgrounds, including Jane Addams of Hull House, whose father was a Congregationalist minister, and Charles R. Henderson and Shailer Mathews,

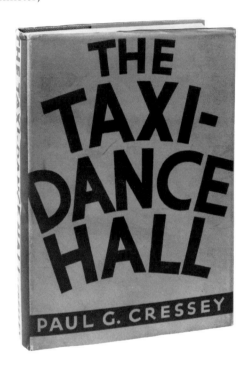

Paul G. Cressey, *The Taxi-Dance Hall: A Sociological Study in Commercialized Recreation and City Life* (Chicago: University of Chicago Press, 1932). "It is a mercenary and silent world — this world of the taxi-dance hall," wrote Paul Cressey in his famous study. "Feminine society is for sale at ten cents a dance."

both clergymen and professors in the University's Divinity School.

For more secular scholars such as sociologists Robert Park and Ernest W. Burgess, Chicago was an ideal subject for systematic research that displayed nearly every human condition compressed into a single, crowded urban mass. In their classic book *The City* (1925), Park and Burgess argued that city life offered all of human society simultaneously, something that scholars investigating isolated tribes in remote locations could never encounter. "The same patient methods of observation which anthropologists like Boas and Lowies have expended in the study of the life and manners of the North American Indian," wrote Burgess, "might be more fruitfully employed in the investigation of the customs, beliefs, social practices, and general conceptions of life in Little Italy on the lower North Side of Chicago."

Drawing on their studies of social conditions in Chicago, Park and Burgess developed generalized theories of urban ecology which explored how cities became divided into separate zones by class and function. They believed that cities had a natural history that, if examined and analyzed, could explain urban cultural patterns. Under the guidance of Park and Burgess, a whole generation of young sociologists explored Chicago to locate problems and populations that could provide data on which to base explanatory models.

The studies produced by these investigators relied on personal contacts between researchers and their subjects. Sociology students were trained to find individuals who typified a particular social problem, a juvenile delinquent or dance hall girl or someone else on the margins of conventional society, and observe and interview them at length. The best of the field research generated by this method was that which captured most fully the life and character of the subjects. In his preface to Clifford Shaw's *The Jack-Roller: A Delinquent Boy's Own Story* (1930), Burgess described the ideal "life-history documents" as microscopes through which to view "the interplay of mental processes and social relationships." Burgess praised Shaw's study, which followed a single delinquent boy for six years, as a "perfect" example of this type of scientific research.

ciency and psychic disturbances; Feeble-minded, moron, diseased brains.

17. THE HOP HEAD.
    The junkie who is addicted to morphine or heroin. The SNIFFER who "whiffs cocaine."
18. THE BUM.
    The drunkard whose life is devoted to securing and consuming alcohol.
19. THE CON.
    The ex-convict.
20. THE GUN.
    The first-class crook who is usually on the road to avoid apprehension.
21. THE YEGG.
    The second-class crook who travels around robbing box-cars, chicken-coops, clothes-lines, etc. *
22. THE JACK ROLLER.
    The individual who makes a specialty of robbing hobos and town workers when they are drunk.
23. THE AGITATOR.
    The individual who travels about organizing the workers and "redeeming the world."
24. THE HIGHBROW.
    The intellectual who is wandering about the country because of biological, psychological, or economic factors.
25. THE DREAMER.
    One who travels about living in a world of poetic dreams and who has a harmonious philosophy that serves as a basis of justification for his living.
26. THE RAMBLER.
    The individual impelled to travel by an active wanderlust. He has a passion to cover extensive territory.
27. THE HOME GUARD.
    The tramp who remains around his home town.
28. THE MISSION STIFF.
    The man who hangs around the missions and gets converted to religion for his bed and board.
29. THE BUNDLE STIFF.
    The hobo who tramps around with his bed and board on his back (the western pioneer type of tramp).
30. THE GRAFTER.
    The man who works the lodges and fraternal orders, or the charity organizations, and fraternity and religious bodies.
31. THE BAD ACTOR.
    One who has disgraced himself and is being paid by his relatives or friends to stay away from home.
32. THE BEACH-COMBER.
    The seaman, sailor, or fireman who loafs about the sea-ports looking for a ship to sign to.

*Sometimes the man who robs by force or stealth his fellows, is known as a hi-jack.

Dr. Ben L. Reitman, "Classification of Tramps, Hobos, and Other Types of Homeless Men," undated. While based largely on his own experience and observation, Nels Anderson's *The Hobo* also drew on information provided by Ben Reitman, a physician who had lived and worked among the homeless of Chicago.

Race and Ethnicity

Another student of Burgess, Nels Anderson, had lived and traveled with hobos before coming to the University to study sociology. As a researcher, Anderson moved into the Madison-Halsted area known as Hobohemia and began interviewing homeless men for their life histories. Afterward, their reminiscences were supplemented with the written records of city welfare agencies so that his subjects' accounts were both verified and enlarged. Anderson's interviews, some running as long as 150 pages, were incorporated into his monograph, *The Hobo: The Sociology of the Homeless Man* (1923).

The intensely personal accounts of individuals collected by the University's sociologists revealed the city of Chicago as a burgeoning metropolis colored by endless hard-luck stories and disturbing verities. The literature of Chicago sociology as it accumulated during the 1920s and 1930s pulsed with vivid tales of drifters, gamblers and hoodlums, domestic strife, sexual vice, the dangers of industrial occupations, the tensions of assimilation, and the powerful undercurrents of group and class.

Ethnic diversity has always been an important element of Chicago's character. Before the Civil War, German, Scandinavian, and Irish immigrants had clustered in separate neighborhoods of the city. In the later nineteenth century, Italians, Poles, Chinese, Greeks, Eastern Europeans, and peoples of other nationalities arrived in Chicago by the thousands and established distinct communities. By the turn of the century and in the years thereafter, a great internal migration brought African-Americans from Mississippi, Alabama, Tennessee, and other southern states to the South Side and West Side of the city.

The first Chicago sociologist to examine one of these ethnic communities in detail was W. I. Thomas, who began graduate work at the University in 1892 and completed his PhD under Albion Small in 1896. With funds provided by Helen Culver, an important benefactor of the University and of Hull House,

"Maxwell Street," from Louis Wirth, *The Ghetto* (Chicago: University of Chicago Press, 1928). Chicago's Maxwell Street and other urban ghettoes, Wirth argued, were both a refuge from prejudice and a continuing cause of social isolation. Woodcut by Todros Geller.

Thomas spent ten years researching Polish society and Polish immigration to America. The results of his study, written in collaboration with Florian Znaniecki, were published in five volumes as *The Polish Peasant in Europe and America* (1918-20). Thomas was particularly concerned with the difficulties of assimilation, describing how the rapid cultural changes encountered in Chicago weakened Polish group cohesion and created an individualism that strained marriages, spurred teenagers to leave home, and led to violence.

The decisive impact of Thomas and Znaniecki's study was due less to the actual data presented than the choice of subject and methodology. Although both Thomas and Znaniecki left the Unversity while the publication of *The Polish Peasant* was still underway, their work set in motion Chicago's strong tradition of ethnic studies. For the Chicago sociologists, the ideal terrain of social analysis lay at points of stress. In showing how individuals or groups deviated from or accommodated to the mainstream, these social scientists hoped to provide data for reforms that would make possible a more complete assimilation of ethnic groups.

Under the guidance of Park and Burgess, an unprecedentedly wide range of race and ethnic studies was produced. Of the fifty-one sociology dissertations written at the University between

THE CHINESE LAUNDRYMAN: A
STUDY OF SOCIAL TYPE

The study of the Chinese laundryman in the city of Chicago and its suburbs is a part of the general study of social type in an American metropolis. It offers a stragic means for getting increased information on the marginal type and the accommodation of such type. The Chinese laundryman recognizably occupies a midway position between that of the native American community and the "Chinatown". His place of business and residence is out side of the Chinese community, m d brings him into contact with native Americans. While this contact is primarily impersonal and commercial in character, it seems, however, to remove him in part from the stream of life of his group. Information already gained seems to indicate that as a result, he occupies an anomalous position, with some interesting effects upon his personality and mode of living. The interest in this study will be then, primarily in analyzing the character of his social situation, the stress which it imposes on him, and the resulting peronality adjustment he makes.

After a year of inquiry, we are now in a better position to arrange a tentatively a schedule, serving as a guide for further search of materials. As the purpose of our study should not be known to the laundrymen, most of the materials obtained are through constant friendly and participant position. Interviews and observations are recorded

Paul C. P. Siu, "The Chinese Laundryman: A Study of Social Type," undated. In examining immigrant acculturation, University sociologists frequently focused on individuals who occupied marginal positions in their own ethnic group.

1919 and 1930, twenty-five related to race and ethnicity, far more than those of any other topic.

Park had accumulated extensive experience of his own in the field. Prior to his appointment to the University faculty, he had served as secretary to Booker T. Washington at the Tuskegee Institute and developed a deep interest in race relations and the culture of African-Americans. In his view, sociology could help accelerate black assimilation into American society.

Park, a former journalist, had also written a book about Chicago's foreign language press. At a time when many Americans regarded the prevalence of immigrant newspapers as a threat, Park interpreted them as a means of further assimilation into the broader society. Later work turned Park again to issues of race relations, which he felt some sociologists were not yet approaching objectively. One of the first sociologists to send students to investigate Chicago neighborhoods troubled by racial conflict, Park viewed racism as an inevitable cycle in human relations, but he believed it would be overcome gradually as society evolved.

Louis Wirth, a student of Park and Burgess, maintained that fundamental research concerning the effects of discrimination and ethnic conflicts could help develop social policy for housing, urban planning, and race relations. In *The Ghetto* (1928), Wirth examined the consquences of centuries of discrimination on Jewish community life, ranging from Renaissance Italy to Chicago's Maxwell Street. *The Ghetto* served as a model for the University's researchers in ethnicity, many of whom later studied under Wirth when he joined the University's faculty.

While most of the studies of race relations were conducted by the whites who made up the bulk of the sociology department, Park, Burgess, and Wirth also attracted a highly capable group of African-American scholars, many of whom were to have distinguished careers in the social sciences. Among them were Charles S. Johnson, America's first professionally trained black sociologist, who later served as president of Fisk University. Another, E. Franklin Frazier, examined the combined issues of family and race in his

1932 study, *The Negro Family in Chicago*. Frazier subsequently taught at Howard University and was elected president of the American Sociological Association in 1948.

As an academic committed to social action, Louis Wirth became involved in numerous groups, committees, and associations concerned with the effects of racial prejudice on community life. He was a founder and president of the Chicago-based American Council on Race Relations, which sponsored research into problems of fair employment, education, housing, and integration. In 1947, with funds from the Carnegie and Rockefeller Foundations, Wirth also established the Committee on Education, Training, and Research in Race Relations at the University of Chicago. Led by Wirth, demographer Philip Hauser, and anthropologist Sol Tax, the committee played a key role in addressing the social and political factors underlying racial discrimination in the city of Chicago.

The Local Setting

Faculty research on urban problems was spurred in 1923 with a grant from the Laura Spelman Rockefeller Memorial for the creation of the Local Community Research Committee. The committee, later renamed the Social Science Research Committee and strengthened by additional grants from the Rockefeller Foundation, was an important source of funding for numerous Chicago-based studies by University sociologists, historians, and political scientists.

The range of this work was apparent in the volume edited by T. V. Smith and Leonard D. White, *Chicago: An Experiment in Social Science Research* (1929). In its first six years, the committee had supported investigations of municipal employment in Chicago, patterns of city development, delinquency and crime, rooming houses, the suburban community, the response of churches to racial issues, the Chicago building trades, parks and recreation, and numerous other subjects bearing on the city. University faculty and graduate students working on committee-funded Chicago research included Park, Burgess, Abbott, Breckinridge, Charles Merriam, Paul Cressey, Norman Hayner, Walter Reckless, and others.

Among those supported by the committee was political scientist Harold F. Gosnell, who fixed his attention on the critical issue of voting behavior. His first study, *Non-Voting: Causes and Methods of Control* (1924), written with Charles Merriam, utilized statistical sampling techniques to examine the drop in voter participation in the 1923 Chicago mayoralty election. Following up with a series of monographs, including *The Negro Politicians: The Rise of Negro Politics in Chicago* (1935) and *Machine Politics: Chicago Model* (1937), Gosnell applied the latest social survey methodologies to an exploration of the city's legendary political topography.

The committee also funded the research of Bessie Louise Pierce, who was brought to Chicago in 1929 as an associate professor of

Harold F. Gosnell, *Machine Politics: Chicago Model* (Chicago: University of Chicago Press, 1937). Like his mentor, Charles Merriam, Gosnell applied quantitative methods to the study of political organizations. He was also influenced by the statistical work of William F. Ogburn, who joined the University's sociology faculty in 1927.

history and head of the History of Chicago Project. Originally conceived as a centennial history of the city, the project was recast by Pierce as a comprehensive survey of all relevant historical records for a definitive history of Chicago from 1673 to 1915. The Field Foundation, Chicago Community Trust, Chicago Historical Society, and Schermerhorn Charitable Trust provided additional support for the project. Working with student assistants, Pierce directed research that produced a compilation of travel accounts, *As Others See Chicago* (1933), and three volumes of *A History of Chicago* (1937-57) describing the city's growth through the conclusion of the Columbian Exposition in 1893. Although the final volume of Pierce's study remained unfinished at her death in 1974, the History of Chicago Project marked an important advance in the development of modern urban history.

The Pattern of Community

As work on the *History* proceeded, Pierce also helped direct the Chicago Foreign Language Press Survey, a project organized in 1936 by the WPA. Under the sponsorship of the Chicago Public Library, the Press Survey located and translated thousands of articles from scores of newspapers published in Chicago's immigrant neighborhoods. More than twenty language communities were represented, from Lithuanian, Slovene, and Filipino to Chinese, Albanian, German, Greek, and Ukrainian. The Press Survey provided important information on the acculturation of recent immigrants and their efforts to assimilate with other groups and American society at large.

Urban geography, demography, and planning are fields in which University researchers have encountered the broadest array of urban issues. Here, as with the more tightly focused studies of the Chicago sociologists, the city was both a convenient setting for research and the embodiment of the tensions and dynamics of the modern metropolis.

One of the earliest University faculty members to become involved in these issues was geographer J. Paul Goode, who served as an "expert investigator" for the Chicago Harbor Commission in 1908-9. Goode visited port facilities in Boston, New York, Philadelphia, and a number of European cities and defined the economic benefits of substantial harbor development in Chicago.

In Goode's deterministic view, Chicago was "A City of Destiny," its population, industry, and wealth a consequence of its physical location at the center of a vast tributary area rich in resources. Speaking before the Geographic Society of Chicago in 1923, Goode predicted that if "industrial and commercial development continue to go along present lines, this great urban vortex ... may well look forward to a population of twelve to fifteen million, before the present century is ended. And there is no discoverable reason why commercial supremacy should ever depart from us."

While not sharing Goode's boosterish enthusiasm, other University scholars joined in the effort to understand Chicago's growth and chart its diverse population. In 1938, the Social Science Research Committee, the National Youth Administration, the Federal Writers' Project, and other sources funded a systematic Chicago survey, the *Local Community Fact Book* (1938). Edited by Louis Wirth and his

"Local Community Research: Studies Completed," Local Community Research Committee, 1929. Within its first six years, the Local Community Research Committee had sponsored more than eighty investigations of urban problems, most of them focusing on Chicago.

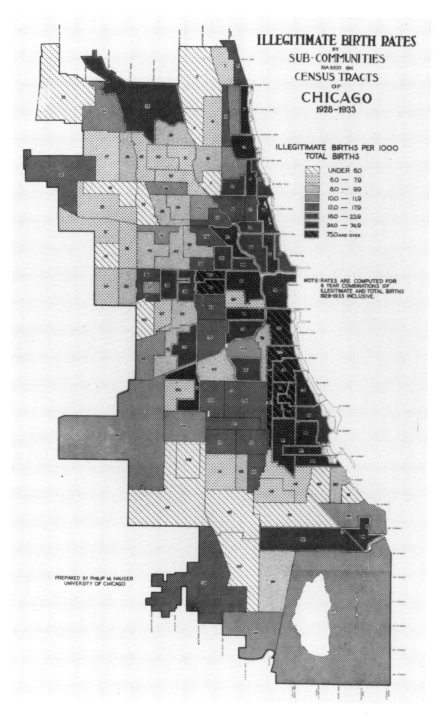

ILLEGITIMATE BIRTH RATES
BY
SUB-COMMUNITIES
BASED ON
CENSUS TRACTS
OF
CHICAGO
1928-1933

ILLEGITIMATE BIRTHS PER 1000
TOTAL BIRTHS

	UNDER 6.0
	6.0 — 7.9
	8.0 — 9.9
	10.0 — 11.9
	12.0 — 17.9
	18.0 — 23.9
	24.0 — 74.9
	75.0 AND OVER

NOTE: RATES ARE COMPUTED FOR
6 YEAR COMBINATIONS OF
ILLEGITIMATE AND TOTAL BIRTHS
1928-1933 INCLUSIVE.

PREPARED BY PHILIP M. HAUSER
UNIVERSITY OF CHICAGO

"Illegitimate Birth Rates by Sub-Communities," map, 1933. Ernest W. Burgess's interests covered nearly every aspect of urban life, particularly those affecting family life. This map was a result of his effort to depict urban trends made evident by census data.

assistant Margaret Furez, the *Fact Book* divided the city into seventy-five distinct communities and developed statistical profiles of each derived from the latest Chicago census data. The information on housing population proved so useful to Chicago public agencies and community organizations that a new *Local Community Fact Book* was published in 1949 and with each decennial census thereafter.

Further development of demographic knowledge of the city was made possible by the work of sociologist Philip Hauser, who studied with Park, Burgess, and their colleague William F. Ogburn, a specialist in statistical methods, before moving through a series of federal census positions and joining the University faculty in 1947. With Evelyn Kitagawa, Hauser edited the 1950 census edition of the *Local Community Fact Book* (1953) and produced studies of statistical standards, population growth, and government policy. A believer in the application of scholarly research to social problems, Hauser was also involved in the Chicago Community Inventory, the Population Research and Training Center, and the Advisory Panel on

Integration in the Chicago Public Schools.

Urban geographer Harold Mayer, another academic in public affairs, joined the Chicago Land Use Survey as a graduate student in geography in 1939. Working under Homer Hoyt, Mayer helped produce a systematic compilation of data and maps identifying land usage throughout the city as well as other studies for the Chicago Plan Commission, including *The Calumet Industrial Area: A Preface to a Comprehensive Development Plan* (1942). Mayer succeeded Hoyt as director of research for the commission from 1948 to 1950, and as a member of the University faculty was later appointed to the Chicago Regional Port District Board. At the request of Mayor Richard J. Daley, he also prepared a comprehensive report on *The Port of Chicago and the St. Lawrence Seaway* (1957).

In contrast to his predecessor Goode, Mayer argued that Chicago was "A City of Decisions," faced with critical choices as it confronted the problems of urban expansion, deterioration of neighborhoods, and the need for integrated transportation systems. "[T]he destiny of a city is not predetermined," Mayer told the Geographic Society in 1955. "Nature offers opportunities. Man decides when and how to utilize them."

Recognizing the need to coordinate graduate training and the research of faculty such as Hauser and Mayer, the University in 1963 formed the Center for Urban Studies. Supported with federal and foundation grants, the center examined individual and family life, the governmental and political process, and the role of the city in economic and cultural change. Urban affairs have also figured in the work of the Committee on Public Policy Studies and in the programs of its successor, the Irving B. Harris Graduate School of Public Policy Studies, established in 1990.

Philip M. Hauser, undated. A scholar with both academic and government experience, Hauser brought demographic expertise to bear on social issues. Photograph by Lewbin Studio.

Settlement and Service

In 1894, the University's Christian Union established the University of Chicago Settlement in the congested immigrant neighborhood southwest of the Chicago stockyards known as the Back of the Yards or Packingtown. Like Hull House, Chicago Commons, and other settlement houses in the city, the University Settlement sought to promote child and adult education, improve working conditions, and help immigrants assimilate effectively into American life. The University offered extension courses and public lectures at Chicago settlement houses, and faculty members such as John Dewey and George Herbert Mead became involved in the conception and direction of settlement programs.

The University of Chicago Settlement League was formed in 1895 as a social and philanthropic organization of University women interested in supporting the work of the University of Chicago Settlement. Led initially by women such as Mrs. William R. Harper, Mrs. Charles Zueblin, and Mrs. Harry P. Judson, the Settlement League was open to female members of the University faculty, wives of faculty members, students, alumnae, and non-University women

committed to the settlement cause. The league staged fund-raising events in support of clubs, classes, and improved facilities at the settlement and programs to promote acculturation of neighborhood residents. League members also worked as volunteers at the settlement, supported legislation for compulsory school

attendance and other reforms, and backed efforts by Mary McDowell, the settlement's head resident, to clean up garbage dumps and build public bathhouses and playgrounds in the Back of the Yards.

The University Settlement never had a formal affiliation with the University, and Mary

FOR THE BENEFIT OF THE
UNIVERSITY SETTLEMENT

A MUSICAL COMEDY IN THREE ACTS
ENTITLED

THE DECEITFUL DEAN

Saturday Evening, March 11, at 8:15 o'clock
STUDENTS' NIGHT — POPULAR PRICES

To be presented by the University of Chicago
Comic Opera Co., in the University Gymnasium,
corner Fifty-Seventh street and Lexington avenue

PATRONESSES

Mrs. Frederic Ives Carpenter	Mrs. George L. Hendrickson
Mrs. Henry Donaldson	Mrs. Robert Morss Lovett
Mrs. Horace Spencer Fiske	Mrs. Adolph Caspar Miller
Mrs. William Gardner Hale	Mrs. Charles F. Millspaugh
Mrs. William R. Harper	Mrs. George E. Vincent
Mrs. Henry R. Hatfield	Mrs. Charles Zueblin
Mrs. George Adams	Mrs. H. H. Kohlsaat
Mrs. Ogden Armour	Mrs. W. R. Linn
Mrs. Samuel E. Barrett	Mrs. Frank O. Lowden
Mrs. A. C. Bartlett	Mrs. Harold McCormick
Mrs. Emmons Blaine	Mrs. Martin Ryerson
Mrs. Chauncey Blair	Mrs. George Seaverns
Mrs. C. W. Brega	Mrs. Byron Smith
Mrs. J. J. Glessner	Mrs. Albert A. Sprague
Mrs. Charles Hutchinson	Mrs. Otho S. A. Sprague
Mrs. Charles Hamill	Mrs. William B. Walker

Mrs. H. M. Wilmarth

Boxes $9.00; Reserved Seats $1.00. Tickets may be had at the University Book Store — Conveyances will be at South Park Station to meet Illinois Central train leaving Randolph Street at 7:30 — Fare ten cents each way

"The Deceitful Dean," University of Chicago Comic Opera Company, announcement, 1899. Theatricals and other benefits sponsored by the University community raised funds for settlement programs.

THE UNIVERSITY OF
CHICAGO SETTLEMENT

Nurse giving a demonstration to a Mothers' Club at the
University of Chicago Settlement

WHAT IS IT ACTUALLY DOING?

WHAT DOES IT AIM TO DO MORE?

University of Chicago Settlement, brochure, 1912.
Infant health, child care, and adult education were
central concerns of settlement workers.

Camp Farr, University of Chicago
Settlement League, brochure, 1943.
The Settlement League sponsored
annual summer outings in Indiana for
children from the crowded Back of
the Yards neighborhood.

McDowell fought successfully to maintain its independence. Through the work of the Settlement League and contacts made by student social workers and faculty, however, the settlement offered members of the early University community what was perhaps their closest contact with poor and working-class Chicagoans. From its initial quarters in a walk-up apartment, the Settlement grew to occupy a substantial complex of buildings on Gross (later McDowell) Avenue, complete with a school and gymnasium. In 1923, league member Shirley Farr helped expand the settlement's program by providing funds for the creation of a permanent summer camp near Chesterton, Indiana.

By the 1950s, the league, renamed the University of Chicago Service League, was dividing its resouces between the settlement and a series of new programs in the University's own community, including support for more than seventy organized youth groups through the Hyde Park Neighborhood Club. The settlement was eventually merged with the Chicago Commons Association and its buildings demolished, but the league continued to maintain an interest in the old stockyards neighborhood through the association's South Side Services Area and the annual summer camp, now known as Camp Brueckner-Farr.

Although he was firmly committed to the virtues of academic research, William R. Harper understood at the founding of the University that scholars could become narrowly preoccupied with their own work and isolated from social realities. Endorsing the creation of the University of Chicago Settlement, he pointed out that the settlement was "not a missionary effort but a necessity to counteract the selfishness of the intellectual life of the University." Support for the social and philanthropic activities of the Settlement League and the Service League represented part of the effort to right the balance.

The training of social workers in Chicago began in 1894, when Graham Taylor, a professor at Chicago Theological Seminary, sponsored a series of lectures at Chicago Commons, the settlement house he had founded. In 1903, Taylor and William R. Harper collaborated in establishing a social work curriculum in the University's Extension Division, but the institutional ties were frail and dissolved quickly after Harper's death in 1906.

Taylor immediately reconstituted his courses under the auspices of the Chicago Commons

and in 1908, with the aid of a grant from the Russell Sage Foundation, founded the Chicago School of Civics and Philanthropy, the nation's first full-time school of social work. Julia Lathrop, a Hull House resident, was recruited to direct training in social survey work, and Sophonisba Breckinridge, a political economist in the University's Department of Household Administration, was brought in as her assistant. Breckinridge was the first woman to complete a PhD in political science at the University and the first woman to

Julius Rosenwald, Sophonisba P. Breckinridge, and Graham Taylor to the Trustees of the University of Chicago, August 4, 1920. The creation of the School of Social Service Administration was accomplished with the participation of Julius Rosenwald, University trustee and Chicago philanthropist.

CHICAGO SCHOOL OF CIVICS AND PHILANTHROPY
2559 MICHIGAN AVENUE

August 4, 1920.

To the Trustees of the University of Chicago:

Gentlemen:

Acting in behalf of the Board of Trustees of the Chicago School of Civics and Philanthropy, we whose names are undersigned are authorized to submit for your consideration the following statement and proposals:

For several years the Chicago School of Civics and Philanthropy has existed for the purpose of providing facilities for the training of students who desire to enter the field of social work and civic service. The work has in the past been to an extent experimental and there have been many groups of students received and cared for.

The most important part of the training, however, has been that provided for college graduates, and the Trustees of the School are convinced that the methods and principles applicable to this portion of their work have been so well developed that it would now be wise to have this graduate training carried on under university auspices rather than under those of a separate organization.

They therefore propose:—

1. That the University of Chicago establish a graduate professional curriculum for training students who desire to enter this field;

2. That in so doing they desire to make it a matter of record that in their judgment such a curriculum can fulfil the demands of the situation only if it be given under conditions of administrative unity characteristic of professional schools, if the classroom work is supplemented by "field work" and skilled placement of graduates, and if the high quality of the student body is assured by the provision of scholarships and fellowships;

3. That the Trustees of the University of Chicago are to regard these proposals as contingent upon the receipt of guarantees of not less than $35,000 a year for the period of five years to be paid to the University of Chicago as may be stipulated.

Signed:

Woodlawn Social Services Center, Hausner & Macsai, architects, J. Lee Jones, associate architect, perspective drawing, 1967. SSA's programs combined rigor in academic research with direct involvement in neighborhood social service.

receive a degree from its Law School. Soon thereafter, Edith Abbott, a Wellesley faculty member who held a University of Chicago doctorate in political economy, joined the staff of the Chicago School.

Although the Chicago School was successful in attracting students, Breckinridge grew frustrated with a curriculum that was limited to vocational training and sources of funding that were increasingly inadequate to meet the needs of the profession.

Encouraged by Julius Rosenwald, a trustee of the Chicago School and a trustee and generous supporter of the University, Breckinridge in 1920 negotiated the basis for a merger of Taylor's school with the University. With Taylor's reluctant endorsement, the training curriculum re-emerged under University auspices as the School of Social Service Administration (SSA), a graduate program providing education in social service techniques but emphasizing profes-

sional studies and a theoretical approach to social issues.

With Edith Abbott as dean, SSA strengthened existing ties within the Chicago social services community and developed new links. Attracted by the school's location and scholarship programs, between a fourth and a third of SSA's student body was drawn from the city of Chicago. Abbott promoted Chicago settings for field research and worked closely with agencies such as United Charities of Chicago in securing placement for graduating students. New specializations such as medical and psychiatric social work were the basis for programs and placements at the University of Chicago hospitals, Cook County Hospital, Children's Memorial Hospital, and other local medical institutions.

Abbott's integration of the SSA curriculum with the social needs of the Chicago community was maintained by her successors following her retirement in 1942. Fieldwork, theses, and monographs by SSA students and faculty continued to emphasize the importance of Chicago as a setting for social analysis and reform. In 1969, following a feasibility study of the need for a clinical field facility and supported by funds from the U.S. Department of Housing and Urban Development, SSA established the Woodlawn Social Services Center. Providing employment services, vocational rehabilitation, youth programs, and early childhood development counseling, the Woodlawn Center marked an effective interaction of academic studies with government policy and the life of a Chicago neighborhood.

In an effort to link the University more closely with the city, and as an expression of his desire for coordination of all levels of American education, William R. Harper in 1896 agreed to serve on the Chicago Board of Education. While on the Board, he headed the Educational Commission which conducted a year-long study into ways to remove the governance of the Chicago public schools from the realm of political patronage. The Commission issued its report in 1898, but its recommendations were blocked by political interests in City Hall. The report was finally approved by the city government in 1917 after several years of school reform under Superintendent Ella Flagg Young, who had studied and taught at the University.

For much of this period, the University of Chicago Laboratory Schools served as an important counterpoint to the educational practices prevailing in the public schools. Though linked most notably with the reputation of John Dewey, the Laboratory Schools were in fact the union of several elementary and secondary educational institutions incorporated within the University at the turn of the century.

In 1896, a University Elementary School was established by

Dewey to serve as a workshop for classroom observation and the testing of educational method; known as the Dewey School or the Laboratory School, it soon attracted national attention and supported Dewey's growing reputation among progressive educators. Five years later, William R. Harper negotiated the acquisition and consolidation of three independent Chicago institutions. Two local secondary schools, the Chicago Manual Training School and the South Side Academy, were merged to form the University High School. The Chicago Institute, a private teachers' college founded by Anita McCormick Blaine in 1899, was incorporated as the College of Education. The institute's elementary school was amalgamated with the University Elementary School and the University Kindergarten.

This massive reorganization gave the University a complete educational system extending from kindergarten to the graduate level which was to have an important influence on the development of education both within the city and nationally. It was not without its casualties, however. Colonel Francis W. Parker, the highly respected educational reformer who was head of the Chicago Institute, died a year after the consolidation. Dewey, whose plans for the School of Education could not be reconciled with Harper's, resigned in 1904 and left for Columbia University. Under Charles H. Judd and William S. Gray, the School of Education shifted its emphasis to fields such as educational psychology and testing, but it continued to influence educators at the elementary, secondary, and college levels.

Many of the Laboratory Schools' central educational tenets were promoted in the Chicago public school system by Ella Flagg Young, one of Dewey's most gifted students. Young came to the University in 1899 at the age of fifty-four with a substantial record of administrative and teaching experience. Within a year she had completed her PhD in education and joined the University faculty, where she developed sixteen new courses, edited a journal for teachers, and administered the Dewey School. After leaving the University in the wake of Dewey's departure, Young went on to become principal of the Chicago Normal School and from 1909 to 1915 the superintendent of the Chicago public schools, the first woman to head a major school system in the United States.

As superintendent, Young initiated a variety of reforms based on her work with Dewey.

Anita McCormick Blaine et al. to the Trustees of the University of Chicago, February 5, 1901. The transfer of the Chicago Institute to the University was a critical element in President Harper's plan for a comprehensive educational program.

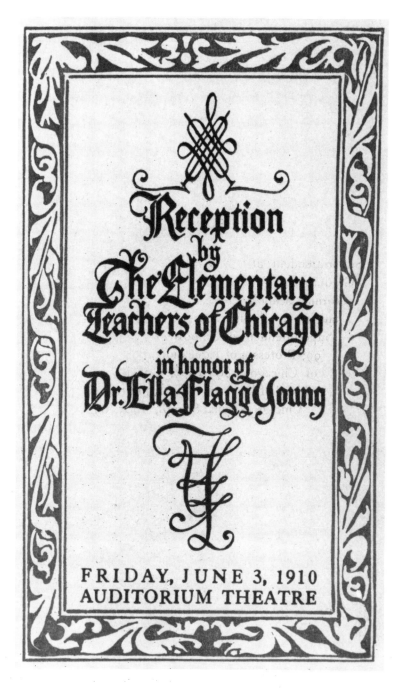

Reception
by
The Elementary
Teachers of Chicago
in honor of
Dr. Ella Flagg Young

FRIDAY, JUNE 3, 1910
AUDITORIUM THEATRE

Among them were the first programs in vocational training and the reorganization of the mathematics and English curricula to replace rote memorization with exercises more directly tied to everyday experience. She also instituted in practice Dewey's theory of democratic education. In a radical departure for an administrator of her time, she encouraged teachers to help shape curricula and operate schools, as was the pattern at the Laboratory Schools. Teacher councils established at Young's direction eventually grew into the Chicago Teachers' Federation. Many of the recent reform efforts in the Chicago public school system, including the establishment of local school councils, mirror Young's commitment to progressive educational ideals.

"Reception by the Elementary Teachers of Chicago in Honor of Dr. Ella Flagg Young," program, June 3, 1910. Chicago teachers honored Ella Flagg Young upon her appointment as public school superintendent.

Science and Medicine

Research Institutes and Accelerator Building under construction, 1951. Within weeks of the end of the war, President Hutchins announced plans for new permanent institutes for scientific research to be built on campus. The buildings were constructed across the street from the old Stagg Field stands, where "CP-1," the first atomic pile, had been built. Photograph by Rus Arnold.

Science in the City

President Harper sought the best men and facilities to support a full complement of scientific programs for the new university. Laboratories, greenhouses, and museums were constructed on the quadrangles, but they were never expected to be large enough to house the activities of University of Chicago scientists. Biologists spent summers at the Marine Biological Laboratory in Woods Hole, Massachusetts; botanists trekked through the lakeshore dunes north and south of Chicago. Bacteriologist Henry Taylor Ricketts traveled to Montana and Mexico to find the source of spotted fever and typhus. James Henry Breasted studied the archaeology of the Near East while Frederick Starr took notes on religious customs and symbols as he made a pilgrimage of the eighty-eight temples of Shikoku in Japan.

Although the University of Chicago's Department of Physics was well known through the work of Albert A. Michelson, Robert A. Millikan, Arthur Holly Compton, and others, the news which broke after atomic bombs fell on Japan in August 1945 brought the University's scientists to new prominence. There could be no hiding the fact that an international team of physicists and engineers had been assembled on campus early in 1942 for top-secret research; but the announcement that Enrico Fermi and his group had built a nuclear pile and successfully initiated the first self-sustaining nuclear reaction, under the football stands, in the heart of the city, stunned even the faculty members who had eaten lunch every day with the physicists in the Quadrangle Club.

The nuclear pile had been planned for a site in the Cook County Forest Preserve, but a construction workers' strike and severe time constraints forced the group to build it on campus. Although the scientists were convinced their safety precautions were adequate, project director Compton wrote later, "I should have taken the matter to my superior. But that would have been unfair. President Hutchins was in no position to judge the hazards involved. Based on considerations of the University's welfare, the only answer he could have given would have been—no. And this answer would have been wrong."

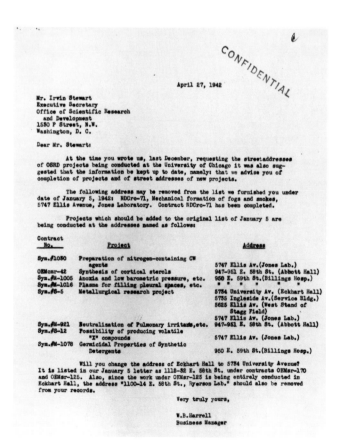

William B. Harrell to Irvin Stewart, April 27, 1942. Under the code name of "Metallurgy," nuclear research was one of many war contracts given to the University by the government's Office of Scientific Research and Development.

"West End of Blue Area Looking Southwest," Argonne National Laboratory, Voorhees Walker Foley & Smith, architects and engineers, predecessor firm of Haines Lundberg Waehler, perspective drawing by Chester B. Price, ca. 1948. Construction of permanent facilities at the Du Page County site began in 1948, and the new laboratories were in full operation by 1953. Photograph courtesy of Argonne National Laboratory.

Work accelerated in October 1942 as problems with equipment and obtaining pure materials were solved one by one. Orders with "double X priority" for graphite, uranium oxide, lumber for scaffolding, and a huge square balloon from Goodyear arrived at the Ellis Avenue laboratory with no questions asked. Youths from the Back of the Yards neighborhood were recruited to assist physics students to machine 400 tons of graphite into bricks and press uranium oxide into 22,000 small spheres.

The Manhattan Project marked a shift in scientific research from privately supported research of individual professors, to massive team projects requiring expensive equipment, sponsored directly by the government. The experience gained in managing huge contracts during the war led to continued cooperation between the government and the University for scientific research and training in subsequent years. Construction soon began on Argonne National Laboratory,

built by the government and operated by the University, to continue experiments with new types of nuclear reactors and technology. The University had chosen a farmland site in Du Page County, and soon the sleepy rural villages of Lemont and Downers Grove experienced a boom as scientists, technicians, and other employees sought housing and services close to their work.

While nuclear research under government sponsorship moved to the suburbs, the University sought industry and corporate support to build facilities for basic research on campus. The Enrico Fermi Institute and the James Franck Institute were outgrowths of efforts in the 1950s to expand facilities and spur research in areas which would eventually be of use to industry and business. Medical uses of radioactive isotopes were explored in the Argonne Cancer Research Hospital on Ellis Avenue. With funding from NASA, the University built the

Laboratory for Astrophysics and Space Research, which provided facilities for University research connected to NASA's space flights.

When government support declined in the 1980s, the University sought better means to connect the long-term goals of its research programs with the needs of businesses and industries which could benefit from its discoveries. Closer relationships needed to be developed to increase commercial dissemination of products and processes derived from laboratory investigations. In 1986 ARCH was created—the Argonne National Laboratory-University of Chicago Development Corporation—to assist in moving scientific discoveries from research laboratories to the marketplace. ARCH coordinated the development of industrial applications from scientific research and, with support from the Graduate School of Business, assisted with venture capital, marketing strategies, and management for commercial spin-offs.

An Urban Research Hospital

By the time the University of Chicago opened in 1892, medicine was finally becoming a modern profession as well as a science. Most medical schools were still privately run, usually by a group of physicians as an extra source of income. As understanding of germ theory and the use of anesthesia spread, medicine became better grounded in scientific principles, and medical research was taken up by universities. The medical school at Johns Hopkins was an early model.

President Harper included departments of anatomy, physiology, and neurology in the University when it opened, and soon added pathology, bacteriology, physiological chemistry and pharmacology. Plans for a medical school were under discussion from an early date, and by 1898 a formal affiliation with Rush Medical College was signed. Students spent their first two years at the University, then two more years at Rush to complete their MD degree.

The affiliation with Rush was always seen as temporary, although it lasted into the 1940s. Rush had a high reputation as a medical school in Chicago, but it did not represent the research-oriented methods sought by the

Mrs. Kellogg Fairbank, President Robert M. Hutchins, Dr. Joseph B. DeLee, and Mrs. Mortimer Singer, Chicago Lying-In Hospital cornerstone laying, November 5, 1929. DeLee established Lying-In as an independent Chicago hospital in 1895 to make modern obstetric methods and sanitation available to indigent mothers. The hospital's low death rates helped convince mothers to give birth in hospitals rather than at home. Affiliation with the University gave the hospital a new building on the Midway, and the Department of Obstetrics and Gynecology was founded with DeLee as head.

University. In 1916 Abraham Flexner of the Rockefeller Foundation, a strong advocate of reform in medical education, reviewed the situation at the University and proposed that the University form its own medical school and hospital. The proposal was expensive but would allow the University to define

and control its program from the ground up.

A total of $5.3 million was quickly pledged after plans were announced in 1916, but the war and escalating building costs stalled the opening of the school and hospital until 1927. The new 200-bed Billings Hospital allowed students to complete their full clinical training on the University campus. The Rush facility was to be used for post-graduate training and research, although those plans were never fulfilled.

The University of Chicago plan was based on the ideas of Flexner along with other physicians at the Rockefeller Institute, which emphasized the need for physicians to be salaried and independent of patient fees. Other university hospitals charged little or nothing to patients who were used in the educational process, but their doctors had private practices "on the side" to make an adequate living. In order to give its physicians full salaries, the University of Chicago had to charge patients regular fees. Using paying patients as teaching subjects was nearly unprecedented, but proved more successful than many anticipated.

Other Chicago institutions soon affiliated with the University, including Chicago Lying-In Hospital, the Country Home for Convalescent Children, the Home for Destitute Crippled Children, the Home for the Incurables, and La Rabida Children's Hospital and Research Center. Each of these added a special focus to the University's program. Recently the hospital expanded its facili-

ties into other parts of the city through an affiliation agreement with Weiss Memorial Hospital on the North Side, the creation of a senior health center at Windermere House in East Hyde Park, and a downtown clinic.

Conceived as a research facility and without the endowment necessary to provide free services to patients, the University of Chicago hospitals and clinics nonetheless provided care to a substantial portion of the South Side population. As other

hospitals on the South Side closed in the 1970s and 1980s, the University accepted larger responsibilities for the health care of those in the surrounding neighborhoods. Balancing this responsibility with the needs of research and teaching has been a constant challenge.

Bobs Roberts Memorial Hospital, pediatric clinic, ca. 1940. The Bobs Roberts hospital treated patients for the Department of Pediatrics until its work was taken over by the Wyler Children's Hospital, which opened in 1967.

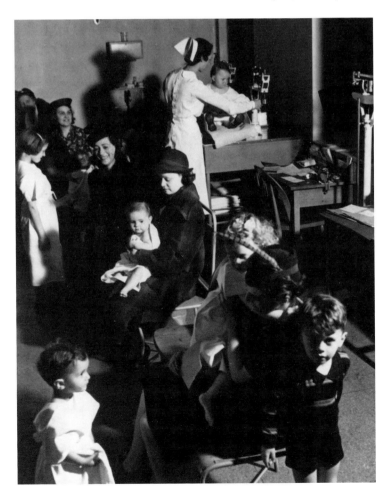

Bringing the University
to the City

Executive Program, Graduate School of Business, class, undated. Photograph by
Stephen Lewellyn (AB 1948).

Professional Schools

With the goal of research always in mind, the University developed schools to train professionals in ministry, medicine, business, education, and law. Schools for music and engineering were also contemplated by President Harper before he died. Chicago graduates found positions nationwide, but a substantial number made their homes in the city and surrounding region. Of 27,000 alumni in the Chicago metropolitan area in 1991, 9000 were MBAs, 2000 worked in the legal professions, 1200 served as social workers, and 800 were physicians.

While the Law School faculty quickly gained a national reputation for its research on broad issues, some professors focused on improving the legal system in Chicago as well. Julian Mack, appointed to the first faculty when the Law School opened in 1902, became a Cook County circuit court judge and helped establish guidelines for the recently established juvenile court. In close association with the Chicago Woman's Club and Hull House, he helped found the Juvenile Protection Association and Immigrants' Protective League and was active in other philanthropic endeavors. Ernst W. Puttkammer, a specialist in criminal law, wrote *A Manual of Criminal Law and Criminal Procedure for Police* (1931) for the Chicago Citizens' Police Committee and served for many years on the Chicago Crime Commission.

For over thirty years Law School students have participated in the Mandel Legal Aid Clinic, which assists indigent clients with cases and allows third-year students to make appearances in state courts. In addition to providing aid to those who cannot afford it, students prepare test cases on recurrent problems in areas such as utilities regulation, government benefits, children's rights, mental health, consumer advocacy, and employment discrimination.

From its beginnings as an undergraduate program, the University's school of business was tranformed in the 1940s into a full graduate institution, which aimed to train scholars as well as skilled entrepreneurs. The Graduate School of Business expanded rapidly and became known for its emphasis on the basic disciplines underlying the business environment. Research and training in management, labor relations, finance, and marketing received sponsorship from Chicago-area firms.

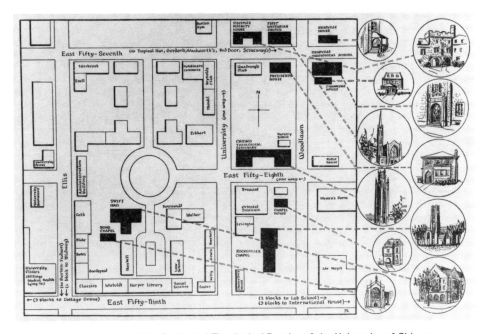

Announcements of the Federated Theological Faculty of the University of Chicago, 1958-1959. The 1943 merger of the faculties of Chicago Theological Seminary, Meadville Theological School, Disciples Divinity House, and the University's Divinity School created the largest group of theological institutions in the nation. Although this joint venture was discontinued in 1960, the schools have continued to work closely under less formal arrangements.

As early as the 1930s, the business school also sponsored downtown programs for working business people. The Executive Program was created for experienced managers who wanted to sharpen their decision-making skills and broaden their understanding of problems which extended beyond individual companies or industries. Likewise, the 190/MBA program provided younger executives with opportunities to study during evenings or weekends while working full-time. Faculty members gained by testing their theoretical assumptions against the experiences of students who were already engaged in commercial activities.

The Divinity School was formed from the Baptist Union Theological Seminary, which had been in operation for twenty-five years before the University opened in 1892. Students from other denominations were welcomed, and by 1894 the Disciples Divinity House opened to support students from that denomination at the University. Ryder Divinity House, associated with Lombard College in Galesburg, Illinois, similarly helped Universalist students.

Harper advocated affiliation agreements with other denominational schools, intending to make the University of Chicago a nucleus for theological and ministry training in the Middle West. At first hesitant to accept Harper's invitation because of the "tainted" Rockefeller money at the University, Chicago Theological Seminary (Congregational) decided to move from its West Side location to Hyde Park in 1914. Meadville Theological School (Unitarian) arrived from Pennsylvania in the 1920s, following a successful exchange program with the University.

More recently, the Lutheran School of Theology at Chicago built a new campus on 55th Street, and McCormick Theological Seminary (Presbyterian) sold its North Side campus to DePaul University and moved into the former Phi Kappa Psi fraternity house at 56th and Woodlawn. The Catholic Theological Union, the largest Roman Catholic theological school in the country, is also located in Hyde Park. This accumulation of theological institutions has not only expanded educational opportunities for students and faculty from many denominations, but has produced a substantial body of ministerial candidates for the Chicago region.

The campus of the University was never meant to contain its educational mission. As conceived by William R. Harper, the University of Chicago included an extension division that would bring instruction to students who could not work toward their degrees on campus. The extension offered three methods of instruction: students could learn

University College, lecture and course leaflets, 1931, 1935, 1936. The University's extension program offered a wide variety of courses and lectures, both downtown and on campus, often in cooperation with other Chicago institutions and organizations.

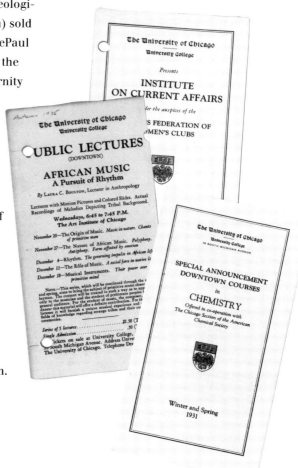

by attending a series of scheduled lectures (lecture-study), register for courses offered in an extension center (class-study), or receive instruction through the mail at home (correspondence-study). At a time when state universities were bound to their rural land-grant campuses and the concept of adult education was still new, the University's offering of extension courses in the city provided opportunities for students for whom conventional higher education was out of reach.

Harper had several models for his extension program. The correspondence-study component of the extension was derived from Harper's own entrepreneurial experience as the founder and promoter of a surprisingly successful Hebrew correspondence school. The inspiration for lecture-study and class-study extension programs came in part from American educational and religious institutions offering similar fare, including the famous summer sessions of Chautauqua which Harper knew personally. It was also shaped by the lecture courses offered through the extension programs at English universities. The British public had attended them so enthusiastically that some of the lecturers were minor celebri-

Basic Program of Liberal Education for Adults, University College, 1954. Basic Program groups met once or twice weekly to discuss writings of more than forty authors including Homer, Joyce, Aeschylus, Racine, Aristotle, and Marx. Photograph by Stephen Lewellyn (AB 1948).

ties. As the administrator and first lecturer for Chicago's program, Harper recruited Richard Green Moulton, Cambridge's most popular extension lecturer. Moulton, who lectured at the University's downtown extension center until 1919, routinely filled the 275-seat auditorium with his addresses on English literature.

Over the years, the University Extension offered both courses for credit and nondegree classes. Correspondence courses were ended in the mid-1960s, but lecture and seminar programs continued. In recent years, the Extension Division, renamed and redefined as the Office of Continuing Education, continues to offer an appealing array of adult education programs.

Enthusiastic response to the University's first half-century of extension courses prepared the way for one of Chicago's best known ventures in continuing education, the Great Books program. In 1943, Wilbur Munnecke, then vice-president of Marshall Field and Company, complained to President Robert M. Hutchins that too many bright businessmen had difficulty communicating. Munnecke thought that a great books discussion group, like the one Hutchins had conducted on campus with Mortimer Adler, would help overcome the problem. The result of this idea was a gathering of top Chicago executives, informally known as the "Fat Men," who met regularly to read and discuss the classic works of the Western tradition. The success of the group was so immediate that the experiment was taken to the Chicago Public Library, where librarians were trained to lead discussions.

Within three years, a citywide Great Books program had been established in Chicago and a number of other cities. A manual for discussion leaders was prepared so that even participants untrained in scholarly criticism could lead lively, informed discussions. In 1946, Hutchins, who had made frequent personal and radio appearances on behalf of the program, established the independent Great Books Foundation with a $132,000 loan from the University.

Great Books continued to grow and thrive. In Chicago, the first major city to embrace the program, public schools have offered Great Books for twenty-five years in over 250 local schools. Today 30,000 adults take part in discussion groups, and nearly one million children are introduced to at least some of its content through public schools and libraries. For its part, the University offers the Basic Program of Liberal Education, a series of continuing education courses centered on reading the classic texts of the Western tradition.

On February 4, 1931, three University of Chicago professors sat around an already antiquated microphone in Mitchell Tower for an unrehearsed discussion of a new government report on prohibition. It was one of the earliest informal, "round table" discussions of a public issue ever heard on radio. To broadcast the program, Chicago station WMAQ had to waive its standing rule against ad-libbing on the air.

That first experiment led to the long-running "University of Chicago Round Table" radio program. In the mid-1930s, WMAQ's parent network, NBC, picked up the program for broadcast nationally on Sunday afternoons. Much of the program's success was due to William Benton, co-founder of the Benton and Bowles advertising agency, a trustee and vice-president of the University, who saw early the power mass media could have in presenting the University to the public.

Benton encouraged President Hutchins to improve the quality of the "Round Table" and expand its reach. By 1951, the "Round Table" was carried by ninety-eight network and twenty educational radio stations and had the largest national audience of any discussion program. Over the

years, participants included public figures such as John F. Kennedy, Ralph Bunche, Jawaharlal Nehru, and Adlai Stevenson as well as a wide range of University faculty from all disciplines.

Although the radio version of the "Round Table" was discontinued in 1955, it was reincarnated as a television program from 1967 to 1974. Chicago's educational television station, WTTW, produced the new "Round Table" initially for the local audience

"The Great Ideas," Round Table transcript, June 11, 1950. Transcripts were prepared for each Round Table broadcast. At the height of the program's popularity, more than 20,000 subscribers received weekly copies.

"Higher Education for All," Round Table, January 25, 1948. Left to right: T. R. McConnell, Louis Wirth, and Earl J. McGrath. T. R. McConnell was a member of President Truman's Commission on Higher Education, which predicted a doubling of college students by 1960. Louis Wirth, a frequent Round Table panelist, called the finding "fantastic."

and then later for distribution to public television stations throughout the Midwest.

The University has made other forays into broadcast media, most of them created for Chicago audiences. After WTTW first came on the air in 1955, the University produced "The Humanities," a thirteen-week, noncredit course broadcast from the station's studios, which were then located in the Museum of Science and Industry. In the 1960s, "University Radio News," broadcast over station WFMT, provided a look at recent developments in University research. Two weekly radio programs, "From the Midway" and "Conversations at Chicago," produced in the 1960s and 1970s, picked up the discussion format pioneered by the "Round Table." As in earlier decades, the University continued to maintain a media presence that helped shape public understanding of its academic programs and the work of its faculty.

With support from the William Benton Foundation, a new venture began in 1983 when radio and television journalists came to campus as Benton Fellows, taking regular University courses in areas of personal interest and participating in special seminars on public policy issues. The six-month program allowed journalists to reflect on issues facing their profession in ways not usually possible under deadline pressure. In 1987 the Benton Broadcast Project initiated plans to develop broadcast treatments for scholarly activities and research projects. One of its first products was "Bastille," an ambitious radio dramatization marking the bicentennial of the French Revolution.

Homer Goldberg, "The Humanities" television program, 1956. Goldberg, an assistant professor of English, gave a blackboard discussion on Chekhov in one of the first programs to air on WTTW. Photograph by Stephen Lewellyn (AB 1948).

The Political Arena

WHY
YOU SHOULD VOTE FOR

CHARLES E. MERRIAM
FOR ALDERMAN

Honest   Experienced   Courageous

Charles E. Merriam, aldermanic campaign
brochure, 1913. After losing the mayoral race in
1911, Merriam won a second term as alderman,
promising to continue his fight against vice and
"spoils politics."

Expertise and Reform

Most of the University's early presidents, including William R. Harper and Harry P. Judson, supported faculty participation in social service organizations, reform groups, and civic boards. Partisan politics were greeted less favorably. The corruption and spoilage of Chicago politics, some University officials feared, would taint the spirit of liberal education. For faculty members Charles Merriam, Paul Douglas, and T. V. Smith, however, electoral politics offered the most direct route to good government. As reformist politicians, they joined the progressive call for "good government," advocating the creation of public agencies that would be administered not by political hacks but by trained experts. They believed that social policy based on research like that conducted in the University's social science departments could rationalize the democratic process and put an end to the waste and corruption of party patronage.

Charles Merriam came to the University in 1900 to teach political science. Merriam's first entree to Chicago politics came in 1905 when he was asked by the reform-oriented City Club of Chicago to conduct a study of municipal revenues. The study was financed by Helen Culver, a progressive philanthropist who had recently donated money for the University's Hull Biological Laboratories. Culver saw Merriam's involvement as a way to align the University community with the efforts of progressive reformers. Merriam's study led to his appointment to the Chicago Harbor Commission, where he familiarized himself with issues of urban planning.

Despite a lack of enthusiasm from President Judson, who was also head of Merriam's academic department, the young political scientist decided to run for alderman on the Republican ticket. In 1909, Merriam won his first term representing Hyde Park in what was then the 7th Ward. Once on the city council, he immediately called for, and headed, a City Commission on Expenditures. There he discovered such widespread graft and other corruption, much of it linked to aldermanic and ward machines, that the council shut off the commission's funding and tried to repress its findings.

Julius Rosenwald, a generous benefactor of the University and progressive causes, financed the continuation of the commission's work and urged Merriam to run for mayor of Chicago in 1911. The ensuing campaign, managed by Harold Ickes (AB 1897, JD 1907), pitted Merriam as a reform Republican against party

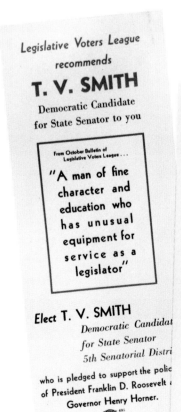

T. V. Smith, state senate campaign brochure, 1934. Smith pledged to support the policies of President Franklin D. Roosevelt and to fight Nazism and religious bigotry.

regulars in Chicago's first direct mayoral primary. Merriam won the nomination, but lost to Carter H. Harrison II in the general election. After a second term in the city council, Merriam ran unsuccessfully in the 1919 Republican mayoral primary on an internationalist platform against isolationist William Hale Thompson.

Later Merriam turned his attention to national politics. In 1931, he helped found the Public Administration Clearing House through which he continued to advocate the role of technical expertise in public service. From 1933 to 1943, Merriam commuted between Chicago and Washington after Harold Ickes, then Secretary of the Interior, enlisted him in the New Deal. With an appointment to the Advisory Committee of the National Planning Board, Merriam helped shape the federal government's first peacetime experiment in national planning.

Thomas Vernor Smith joined the philosophy faculty immediately after receiving his PhD from the University in 1922. He was a founder and a favorite guest of the University of Chicago "Round Table" radio program. Smith spoke frequently about the promise of democracy and advanced his ideas in popular

books, articles, and media appearances. Smith's eloquence appealed to voters, who elected him in 1934 to the state senate as a Democrat from the fifth district, which surrounded the University. While in the Illinois Senate, he advocated reforms of the legislative process and founded the Illinois Legislative Council, an association through which legislators could exchange views on legislative and administrative reforms.

In 1939 Smith was elected to the U.S. Congress as an at-large representative from Illinois, overcoming vigorous opposition from the Kelly-Nash Democratic political machine in Chicago. In Congress, Smith refused an appointment to the powerful Foreign Affairs Committee, saying "I know nothing about foreign affairs." He accused other representatives of "out-talking their information," and pledged to be a "noiseless congressman." Smith chose to sit on the low-profile Civil Service Committee, where he urged that government agencies be run by trained experts familiar with quantitative methods. In his call for a corps of dedicated and efficient public servants, Smith the Democrat echoed many of the long-held positions of his Republican colleague Merriam.

Political figures with University associations have shared a common commitment to honest and effective government. They have also frequently maintained independent postures within one of the two major political parties and received support from non-partisan citizens' groups.

One of the most important of these independent-minded

PLATFORM
of
PAUL H.
DOUGLAS
INDEPENDENT CANDIDATE FOR ALDERMAN
for a —
FINER 5ᵀᴴ WARD
and a —
GREATER CHICAGO

Paul H. Douglas, aldermanic campaign platform, 1939. In his platform, Douglas called for efficient city administration, relief for the poor, and a city board of mediation and arbitration to reduce labor disputes.

politicians was Paul Douglas, professor of economics at the University, who like Charles Merriam began his political career as a Hyde Park alderman. Douglas's studies of wages, particularly his book, *Real Wages in the United States* (1930), had given him some renown as an economist. Most Chicagoans, however, came to know him in 1929 when Douglas headed an investigation of Samuel Insull, Chicago's powerful utilities boss, which resulted in Insull's indictment over improper bond financing schemes. Throughout the 1930s, Douglas served on a variety of local, state, and federal commissions which related more directly to his academic work on wages. More importantly, Douglas helped draft the national Social Security Act of 1935.

Douglas began his aldermanic career in 1939 as the candidate of Mayor Ed Kelly's Democratic machine. But he, like Merriam, soon alienated party regulars by exposing graft and conflicts of interest in the city council. With the support of state progressives, Douglas launched a campaign for the U.S. Senate in 1942, which he lost to the machine candidate.

After the campaign, Douglas, at age fifty, enlisted in the U.S. Marines. He was wounded in Okinawa and spent a year in military hospitals before returning to the University. In 1948, he ran for the U.S. Senate again and won. Douglas served for three terms as a highly respected and independent liberal Democrat. He was defeated in 1966 by Republican Charles Percy (AB 1941), a University of Chicago trustee who also became known for the independent position he occupied within his political party.

Hyde Park's tradition of political independence, starting with Charles Merriam's terms in the city council, has regularly drawn strength from within the University community. Most elected officials from Hyde Park since 1950 have had both University connections and independent political convictions. They include State Representatives Robert E. Mann (MBA 1953, JD 1956) and Barbara Flynn Currie (AB 1968, AM 1973), State Senator Richard Newhouse (JD 1961), Congresswoman Emily Taft Douglas (wife of Paul Douglas and daughter of Lorado Taft, AB 1919), and Aldermen Robert Merriam (son of Charles, AM 1940), Abner Mikva (later congressman, JD 1951), Leon Despres (PhB 1927, JD 1929), Lawrence Bloom (AB 1965, JD 1968), and Toni Preckwinkle (AB 1969, MAT 1977).

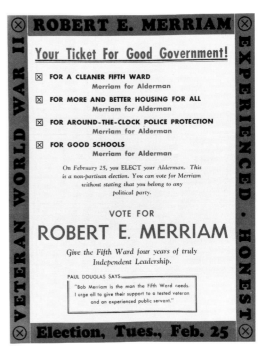

Robert E. Merriam, aldermanic campaign leaflet, 1947. Following in his father's footsteps, Merriam served two terms as alderman for Hyde Park, then lost a close race for mayor in 1955 to Richard J. Daley.

Chicago's good-government organizations, especially the Independent Voters of Illinois (IVI), have long found support from within the University community for their challenges to Chicago's machine politics. The Fifth Ward Committee, an IVI affiliate in the 1950s, was headed by a board of forty-three directors, twenty-one of whom were associated in some way with the University. From the election of Robert Merriam in 1947 and Leon Despres in 1955 to the present, nonmachine candidates have achieved repeated success in Hyde Park and helped sustain the distinctive political culture of the University and its community.

The Civic Spirit

Art Institute of Chicago, Grant Park, 1914. Trustees of the Art Institute cooperated in building a hall for the congresses held in conjunction with the World's Columbian Exposition in 1893, and after the conclusion of the fair used it to house the growing art collections.

An Era of Institution-Building

Although the impetus for the University's creation came from the Baptist churches of Chicago and the Middle West, along with an endowment from John D. Rockefeller, its growth and expansion depended heavily on local businessmen and their families. By the 1890s Chicago business had come of age, and a generation of merchants and financiers were turning their attention to building cultural institutions in the city. As Chicago's literary magazine, the *Dial*, proclaimed, "the signs are clear that the season of mere physical life is over, and that the life of the soul calls for exercise and nourishment." Men who came together to sponsor the World's Columbian Exposition learned to cooperate on other ventures, including the Art Institute, the Chicago Symphony Orchestra, and a new university.

The University of Chicago was one of many institutions created or enlarged in the 1890s. Older organizations such as the Historical Society and the Academy of Sciences had been formed by and for members of genteel society who valued culture; now the emphasis was on institutions which could raise the standards of the public at large. The University's role was

to promote the finest scholarship in all fields of human knowledge.

Martin A. Ryerson and Charles L. Hutchinson served concurrently for nearly three decades as president and treasurer of the University's Board of Trustees.

Sons of pioneer Chicago entrepreneurs, they were especially concerned with bringing refinement and "civilization" to a city which still had the rough face of a frontier town. Through an interlocking series of boards and

University of Chicago faculty petition to the Orchestral Association, March 10, 1894. Sixty-nine faculty members expressed their support for the recently established Chicago Orchestra, insisting it was important for art and education, not merely a "popular entertainment." Signers came from all parts of the University, including zoologist Charles Otis Whitman, mathematician Eliakim Hastings Moore, Divinity School professor Rabbi Emil G. Hirsch, dean of women Marion Talbot, and football coach Amos Alonzo Stagg.

Field Columbian Museum, Jackson Park, undated. The Fine Arts Building for the World's Columbian Exposition continued in use as the first home of the Field Columbian Museum, later renamed the Field Museum of Natural History. When the Field Museum moved to a new site at the south end of Grant Park, the building was refurbished and reincarnated as the Museum of Science and Industry.

committees, Ryerson and Hutchinson with their friends sponsored churches, asylums, hospitals, museums, libraries, schools, and all the other accoutrements Chicago needed to become a world-class city.

Hutchinson inherited his father's holdings in the Chicago Packing and Provision Company, the Chicago Board of Trade, and the Corn Exchange Bank. A conservative investor, he was widely trusted by other businessmen. His travels to Europe convinced him that Chicago should be improved with artworks and other public institutions to raise people's consciousness of higher ideals. Hutchinson spent much

of his time and nearly half his income on philanthropic endeavors, helping to found the Art Institute and later serving as its president; serving as a director of the World's Columbian Exposition and the Chicago Relief and Aid Society, trustee of Presbyterian Hospital, Chicago Lying-In Hospital, and Hull House, treasurer of the Immigrants' Protective League, and president of the Chicago Orphan Asylum; and helping to secure a site for the Field Museum of Natural History. Active in the Commercial Club, Hutchinson also helped organize the Chicago Athletic Club and the Cliff Dwellers, all the while also being an active

member of St. Paul's Universalist Church.

Taking over his father's lumber business, Martin A. Ryerson shared Hutchinson's vision of the ideal city and worked closely with him through much of his life. An avid collector and student of art, he served as vice-president of the Art Institute and of the Field Museum and also supported the Chicago Orphan Asylum, the Sprague Memorial Institute, the Chicago Symphony Orchestra, and *Poetry* magazine. Ryerson had funded the physics laboratory for the University, and his high-minded approach to science was expressed in his speech at the

Merchandisers and Advertisers

dedication of the Yerkes Observatory in 1897, when he encouraged "the cultivation of science for its own sake" at a time when so much energy was expended on "the improvement of material conditions."

University fundraisers sometimes had to compete with counterparts from other organizations. In a sense, though, each institution lent prestige to the others, as each benefited the city as a whole. William R. Harper sought close associations with other educational organizations in the city. Some affiliated directly, such as Rush Medical College, the Chicago Manual Training School, and many years later the John Crerar Library; some discussed mergers or cooperative ventures but remained independent, as did the Armour Institute of Technology and Theodore Thomas's Chicago Orchestra. Others maintained close ties through individual trustees or faculty members, as did the Art Institute and Field Museum. Interaction among the city's educational and cultural institutions strengthened them individually and collectively, as each developed a unique identity and purpose.

Early settlers in Chicago foresaw its geographical potential as a center for trade. Farmers needed supplies from the East and a way to deliver their goods to the proper markets. Chicago was a connecting point for both land and water transportation routes and soon became a hub of retail and wholesale merchandising, as well as a collection point for grain, cattle, and lumber from throughout the Middle West.

University benefactors founded and ran many of Chicago's great retail establishments, including Marshall Field's, Carson Pirie Scott & Co., Mandel Brothers, Wieboldt's, Goldblatt's, Walgreen's drug stores, mail-order giants Sears, Roebuck and Montgomery Ward's, as well as hardware and railroad supply companies. "Not known as a great giver," Marshall Field donated land and sold additional parcels for the original site of the University and later initiated

Carson Pirie Scott & Company advertisement, *Cap and Gown*, 1905. Andrew MacLeish joined the firm of Carson Pirie Scott in 1866. Active in the Fourth Baptist Church, MacLeish had been a trustee of the Old University of Chicago and was one of the original trustees that met to organize the new university in 1890.

a challenge grant that raised $1,000,000 in endowment. Thomas W. Goodspeed, who was responsible for much of the University's fundraising, said that "the University did an equally great service for Mr. Field," opening his eyes to the benefits of philanthropy and leading to other gifts, especially for the creation of the Field Museum.

Julius Rosenwald, president of Sears, Roebuck & Co. during its meteoric rise at the turn of the century, became even better known as a philanthropist, believing in "giving while you live" rather than establishing permanent trusts. He sponsored schools for African-Americans in

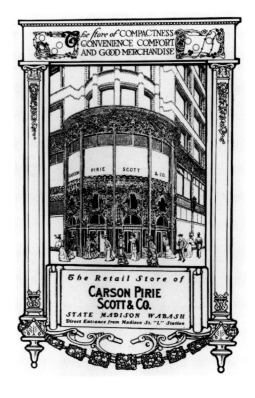

President Max Mason and Mr. and Mrs. William A. Wieboldt, Wieboldt Hall ground-breaking, 1925. The Wieboldt Foundation provided funds for a building to house the University's modern language departments.

rural areas throughout the South and raised money for YMCA buildings in urban areas, as well as aiding the University of Chicago, the Associated Jewish Charities, and the Museum of Science and Industry.

Adolphus Clay Bartlett moved to Chicago in 1863 and took up the hardware business. His main philanthropic interest was the Chicago Home for the Friendless. He became a close friend of William Rainey Harper and a trustee of the University. Bartlett donated funds for the men's gymnasium on campus named for his son, and another son, Frederic Clay Bartlett, painted the interior murals depicting a medieval tournament.

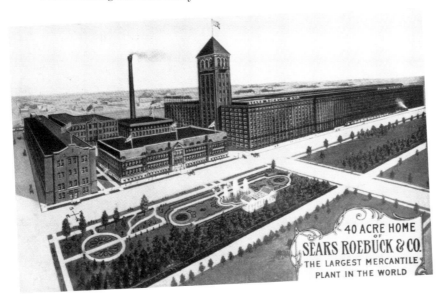

Sears, Roebuck & Company Headquarters, postcard, undated. Built in 1905, the sprawling West Side complex served as the company's main office for sixty-seven years, until the Sears Tower was completed downtown.

Industrialists

Executives from the advertising industry also took an interest in the University. Albert Lasker of the Lord and Thomas agency provided an important endowment for the hospital in its early years, and one of his employees, Fairfax M. Cone, who took over the company renamed as Foote, Cone and Belding, served the University years later as a member and chairman of the Board of Trustees. After deciding to leave his successful career at the New York advertising agency of Benton and Bowles, William Benton accepted the invitation of his Yale classmate, Robert Hutchins, to come to the University of Chicago and study its public relations problems. A confidential report was printed for the trustees which incorporated advice on the latest advertising and promotional techniques. Benton advocated better use of radio broadcasting and films to disseminate the University's name and improve its image. Benton also acquired the *Encyclopaedia Britannica* from Sears and turned over much of its stock to the University, providing an ongoing source of funds from royalties, and initiating a long relationship with *EB* that placed many faculty members in editorial positions.

As trade and transportation lines converged in Chicago, the city became a center for manufacturing and industry of all kinds. Raw materials flowed in by ship from the Great Lakes and by railroad from the surrounding prairie states, and finished goods were sent to both coasts and around the world. The University was a natural beneficiary of successful entrepreneurs who wished to show their civic pride.

As a fiftieth-anniversary brochure declared, "The regular dividends paid by a university are paid to all humanity, in new knowledge, new science, new medicine. The 12,000 Chicagoans who have invested money in the University of Chicago expected nothing more than these regular dividends."

Meat packer Gustavus F. Swift subscribed $1000 for the new University of Chicago in 1890.

Chicago Union Stock Yards, undated. The central stock yard created in 1865 covered 345 swampy acres on the South Side, and included 2300 separate livestock pens as well as hotels, saloons, restaurants, and offices for merchants and brokers.

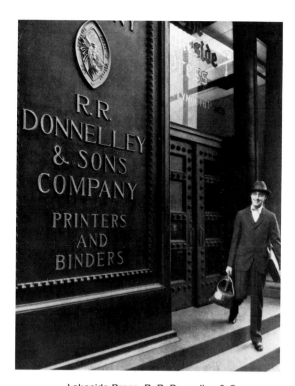

Lakeside Press, R. R. Donnelley & Sons Company, entrance, from *Training Craftsmen at the Lakeside Press* (Chicago: Lakeside Press, 1927). The University's relations with one of Chicago's foremost printing establishments began when R. R. Donnelley became treasurer of the University Press in 1892. His son Thomas served as a trustee and consulted on matters concerning the Press, and grandson Gaylord continued the family tradition as chairman of the Board of Trustees from 1970 to 1976. Photograph courtesy of R. R. Donnelley & Sons Company.

But his most important legacy to the University was certainly his son Harold, who graduated with a PhB in 1907 and became one of the University's most devoted alumni. Chairman of the Board of Trustees from 1922 to 1949, Harold Swift may have spent as much time with University affairs as he did with the family business.

Other meat packers aided the University, including Sidney Kent, an original incorporator of the Union Stock Yards, and Charles Hutchinson, whose father was a partner with Kent in the Chicago Packing and Provision Company. Philip D. Armour, who arrived in Chicago the same year as Gustavus Swift, invested in the Armour Institute of Technology, which later became the Illinois Institute of Technology. Although the two

schools discussed affiliating at several different times, the Armour family preferred to keep their school independent. They did provide for the University in other ways, including the Armour Clinical Research Laboratory in the hospital complex.

Benefactors of the University included manufacturers of lumber, steel, railroad freight cars, steam radiators, farm machinery, electrical equipment, and paper products. Silas R. Cobb, a harness maker who arrived in Chicago in 1833, made enough money to retire in 1852 at the age of 40, and although somewhat intimidating to the University's campaign solicitors, was happy to contribute funds for the University's first lecture hall. Cyrus Hall McCormick, who made Chicago a center for farm implement manufacturing, died

S. S. *Edward L. Ryerson* at Indiana Harbor Works dock, 1960. Inland Steel named the largest ship on the Great Lakes for its retired chairman. Photograph by Inland Steel Company.

Finance and Commerce

before the University opened, but several family members took an active interest in it, including his daughter, Anita McCormick Blaine, who funded the Chicago Institute, which was to become part of the University's College of Education, and her brother Harold, who served as a trustee for many years.

La Verne Noyes was an inventor of farm machinery and also developed a wind-driven motor which could generate electricity. President of the Civic Federation of Chicago, trustee of the Lewis Institute, life-member of the Art Institute, and president of the trustees of the Chicago Academy of Sciences, he donated money for a women's building at the University of Chicago as a memorial to his wife, Ida Noyes, who died in 1912.

Chicago's steel industry was represented at the University by Edward L. Ryerson, grandson of a hardware and steel merchandiser who came to Chicago in 1842. Ryerson served as chairman of Joseph T. Ryerson and Son and later of Inland Steel after the two companies merged; he was chairman of the University's Board of Trustees from 1953 to 1956, and also served for some years as president of the Orchestral Association.

Some fortunes were made in Chicago by speculation, others by careful and sound investments. Early settlers who made good put their money in real estate, banks, railroads, and utilities. Fortunes were as quickly lost as gained in the turbulent economy of the late nineteenth century, subject to panics as well as booms, not to mention the great Chicago fire.

Trusted businessmen played key roles in gaining wide acceptance of the new University. Charles Hutchinson, president of the Corn Exchange Bank, which handled much of the business of the Board of Trade, was one of the first to give his approval to the fundraising campaign of the American Baptist Education Society. In later years, Norman Wait Harris (founder of Harris Trust & Savings Bank) and John Nuveen also lent their support.

Annie McClure Hitchcock, whose family came to Chicago in 1837, provided funds for a men's dormitory at the University in honor of her husband Charles, a founder of the Chicago Bar Association. John P. Wilson, another prominent Chicago attorney, helped guide the University as a trustee in its early

Charles L. Hutchinson in the Roman Forum, 1904. Hutchinson traveled frequently to Europe to study and collect art. Along with his friend Martin A. Ryerson he helped choose English Gothic as the architectural style for the University quadrangles.

Jonathan Young Scammon arrived in Chicago in 1835. A lawyer and banker, he wrote the original ordinances to set up the public schools, helped found the Chicago Historical Society and Chicago Academy of Sciences, donated ground for the Hahnemann homeopathic hospital, and funded an astronomical observatory at the Old University of Chicago campus. Financially ruined by the Chicago fires in 1871 and 1874, he retired to his wife's twenty-acre estate in Hyde Park. Through bequest and purchase, the Scammon property became the site of the Laboratory Schools of the University of Chicago.

Family names such as Searle, Crown, Pritzker, Wyler, Regenstein, Kersten, Mitchell, Pick, and Rubloff represent the wide variety of business interests in the Chicago area which have provided strong support for the University in recent years. A private institution often associated more closely with a national or international community of scholars than with its closer neighbors, the University of Chicago nonetheless relies as it always has on continuing relationships with the citizens, businesses, and institutions of the city to move its work forward.

years. The Chicago legal community provided two chairmen for the Board of Trustees, Laird Bell (1949-53) and Glen A. Lloyd (1956-63).

Gifts came to the University from many types of donors, including the widow of "Diamond Jo" Reynolds, who ran steamboats on the Mississippi River and gold mines in Arizona; Charles T. Yerkes, who created a furor by monopolizing the Chicago street railways; and Helen Culver, perhaps Chicago's first businesswoman, who managed her cousin's extensive real estate holdings and eventually turned many of them over to philanthropic interests, including Hull House (which occupied her family estate), and the University's biological laboratories.

Eli B. Williams came to Chicago in 1833, built a store on South Water Street, and made his fortune from investments in real estate and public utilities. In 1916 his son, Hobart W. Williams, distributed the family properties to St. Luke's Hospital, the Chicago YMCA, and the University of Chicago. The University received the old Williams homestead on Wabash and Monroe, which by then was a valuable commercial block. Sale of the property provided funds to expand the business school.